The
Deeper Wound

DEEPAK CHOPRA

The Deeper Wound

RECOVERING THE SOUL FROM
FEAR AND SUFFERING

RIDER

LONDON • SYDNEY • AUCKLAND • JOHANNESBURG

7 9 10 8 6

First published in 2001 by Harmony Books,
an imprint of Crown Publishing Group, Random House Inc., USA
This edition published in 2001 by Rider,
an imprint of Ebury Press, Random House,
20 Vauxhall Bridge Road, London SW1V 2SA
www.randomhouse.co.uk

Random House Australia (Pty) Limited
20 Alfred Street, Milsons Point, Sydney,
New South Wales 2061, Australia

Random House New Zealand Limited
18 Poland Road, Glenfield,
Auckland 10, New Zealand

Random House South Africa (Pty) Limited
Isle of Houghton, Corner of Boundary Road & Carse O'Gowrie,
Houghton 2198, South Africa

The Random House Group Limited Reg. No. 954009

Design by Lauren Dong

The Random House Group Limited supports The Forest Stewardship Council (FSC),
the leading international forest certification organisation. All our titles
that are printed on Greenpeace approved FSC certified paper carry the FSC logo.
Our paper procurement policy can be found at www.rbooks.co.uk/environment

Printed and bound by Mackays of Chatham PLC, Chatham, Kent

A CIP catalogue record for this book is available from the British Library

ISBN 978-0-7126-5472-2

For Ruth and Paige and Juliana

ACKNOWLEDGMENTS

I WOULD LIKE to take this opportunity to thank the following people: my editor, Peter Guzzardi, who worked tirelessly and impeccably to bring this text to its completion; Linda Loewenthal, who first came up with the idea for this book; Shaye Areheart, Chip Gibson, Tina Constable, and Rhoda Dunn at Harmony Books and Crown Publishers, who have always supported me; Carolyn Rangel, without whom my life would be totally chaotic; Paulette Cole, for her great courage and her commitment to exploring the deeper wound in the face of tragedy; Richard Perl, for supporting Paulette and me; and finally, my family, who nurture me with their love and affection in every moment.

CONTENTS

I know the day will come
When my sight of this world shall be lost.
Life will take its leave in silence,
Drawing the last curtain before my eyes.
Yet stars will still shine at night,
And mornings rise as before,
And hours will still heave like sea waves,
Casting up pleasures and pains.
When I think of this end of my moments
The barrier of the moment breaks,
And I see by the light of death
Your world with its careless treasures.
Rare is its meanest of lives,
Rare is its lowliest seat.
Things that I longed for in vain,
And things that I got—let them pass.
Let me but truly possess
The things that I ever spurned and overlooked.

—Rabindranath Tagore, 1913

PREFACE

ON SEPTEMBER 11, 2001, as fate would have it, I was leaving New York on a jet flight that took off 45 minutes before the unthinkable happened. By the time we landed in Detroit, chaos had broken out. When I grasped the fact that American security had broken down so tragically, I couldn't respond at first. My wife and son were also in the air, on separate flights, one to Los Angeles, one to San Diego. My body went absolutely rigid with fear. All I could think about was their safety, and it took several hours before I found out that their flights had been diverted and both were safe.

Strangely, when the good news came, my body still felt as if it had been hit by a truck. Of its own accord it seemed to feel a far greater trauma that reached to the thousands who would not survive and the tens of thousands who would survive only to live through months and years of hell. And I asked myself, why didn't I feel this way last week? Why didn't my body go stiff when innocent people died through violence in other countries? Around the world my horror and worry are experienced by others every day. Mothers weep over horrendous loss, civilians are bombed mercilessly, and refugees are ripped from any sense of home or homeland. Why did I not feel their anguish enough to call a halt to it?

As we hear the calls for tightened American security and a fierce military response to terrorism, it is obvious that none of us has any answers. However, we feel compelled to ask some questions.

Everything has a cause, so we have to ask, what was the root cause of this evil? We must find out not superficially but at the deepest level. There is no doubt that such evil is alive all around the world and is even celebrated.

Does this evil grow from the suffering and anguish felt by people we don't know and therefore ignore? Have they lived in this condition for a long time?

One assumes that whoever did this attack feels implacable hatred for America. Why were we selected to be the focus of suffering around the world?

All this hatred and anguish seems to have religion at its basis. Isn't something terribly wrong when jihads and wars develop in the name of God? Isn't God invoked with hatred in Ireland, Sri Lanka, India, Pakistan, Israel, Palestine, and even among the intolerant sects of America?

Can any military response make the slightest difference in the underlying cause? Is there not a deep wound at the heart of humanity? If there is a deep wound, doesn't it affect everyone? If all of us are wounded, will revenge work? Will punishment in any form toward anyone heal the wound or aggravate it?

Will an eye for an eye, a tooth for a tooth, and a limb for a limb leave us all blind, toothless, and crippled?

Tribal warfare has been going on for thousands of years and has now been magnified globally. Can tribal warfare be brought to an end? Is it possible, as we move into the future, that all of us, regardless of our race, religion, or even nationality, can transcend our tribal nature?

What are you and I as persons going to do about what is happening? Can we afford to let the deeper wound fester any longer?

This was a horrible attack on America, but is it not also a rift in our collective soul? Isn't this an attack on civilization from without that is also from within?

When we have secured our safety once more and cared for the wounded, after the period of shock and mourning is over, it will be time for soul searching. I only hope that these questions are confronted with the deepest spiritual intent. None of us will feel safe again behind the shield of military might and stockpiled arsenals. There can be no safety until the root cause is faced. It is imperative that we pray and offer solace and help to each other. In this moment of deep sorrow for the wounding of our collective soul, the only healing we can accomplish as individuals is to make sure that our every thought, word, and deed nurture humanity.

Although the idea for this book was born out of the tragic incident on September 11, 2001, the intent of this book evolved so that it has become a manual that can be used to heal the deeper wound no matter what the cause. Great wisdom traditions tell us it is possible to go beyond suffering to reach expanded states of awareness where our personal transformation can not only bring joy to us but also heal the larger web of life. It is my hope that as you create the state of spontaneous joy for yourself by reaching into the depths of your soul, you will also contribute to the restoration of harmony in the world. Because you are the world.

A principle of physics states "When an electron vibrates, the universe shakes." Let us then, you and I, be those electrons that vibrate at the level of consciousness to bring peace, harmony, joy, and love to the world.

INTRODUCTION

MY NAME IS Gotham Chopra, and I am Deepak Chopra's son. I work as a TV reporter with Channel One News, the educational broadcast seen in an estimated 12,500 secondary schools.

At 8:00 A.M. on Tuesday, September 11, I boarded a flight in New York headed for Los Angeles. A few minutes later we lurched back from the gate, fired down the runway, and soared into the sky. It must have been almost 8:30 A.M. when I looked over my shoulder and gazed out at the New York skyline, noting the clear view, from Columbia University, my alma mater, all the way down to the World Trade Center.

"What a beautiful day," I thought to myself. "I wish I wasn't leaving." I then closed my eyes and drifted off to sleep.

A little over 90 minutes later I awoke when the pilot's voice came over the loudspeaker. "Ladies and gentlemen," he announced in a calm voice, "we are making an emergency landing in Cincinnati because of an apparent terrorist attack in the New York area. Please stay calm. . . ."

There was a nervous murmur throughout the cabin. The journalist in me demanded immediate information and I reached for the phone. I quickly ran my credit card through the phone, waited for the dial tone, and dialed my news desk in Los Angeles. The phone crackled but there was no mistaking the panicked tone of one of my colleagues.

"Are you okay?" she asked.

"I am." I asked for further information.

"Two planes crashed into the World Trade Center. They've collapsed. They've come down. . . ."

The phone went dead. I frantically redialed.

No luck.

I tried my sister in Los Angeles.

No luck.

I slowly sat back in my chair and began to panic. I knew my father had flown out of New York on a different flight about an hour before me. I knew my mother was on a flight originating in London destined for San Diego. I tried to meditate and tell myself that everyone would be okay. Tears burned my eyes.

When we touched down twenty minutes later, the pilot instructed us not to turn on our cell phones. He gave us instructions to immediately evacuate the plane and follow the instructions of security personnel.

Finally in the terminal, I reached for my phone and turned it on. There I stood huddled with hundreds of other stranded passengers staring up at the television. There the images of two smoldering stumps—the remains of the towers of the

World Trade Center—played on the screen. Finally I got in touch with my sister, Mallika, who was sobbing on the other end of the phone.

"I'm okay.... Where's Papa? ... Where's Mom?"

Mallika supplied all of the answers—everyone was safe. I placed my next call to the office. I knew that there was work at hand. Sure enough, a car had already been reserved for my return to New York. At the rental agency, people in the long line started shouting out their destinations and everyone began carpooling. I joined two other men from the New York area and we were off. Over the next 12 hours we listened closely to the radio as details of the terrorist attack emerged. Every five minutes the name of another family member or friend popped into my head and I dialed the number frantically. Most New York numbers were jammed or out of service. One friend I was able to reach informed me that he had been unable to contact a mutual friend of ours who worked on the 105th floor of one of the towers. He was scheduled to attend an 8:30 meeting. Someone from the meeting had called to say they had survived the initial attack and were waiting for a rescue team. No one had heard from any of them since.

Finally, just after midnight we made it to Fort Lee, New Jersey, at the edge of New York City. There would be no crossing into Manhattan tonight—all the bridges and tunnels had been sealed. I spent the night in New Jersey unable to sleep much and by 6:00 A.M., I was dressed and ready. The only way to get across was via the commuter train, which was offering limited services. As we pulled into the station in Hoboken, New Jersey, the train slowed to a stop. There on the other side of the river they stood, like ashen smoking gravestones, the ruins of the twin towers. The train was utterly silent as everyone stood and gazed out the window. A young woman beside me began to whimper. Another man lowered his head into his hands to muffle his sobs.

Once in the city, I saw people walking around in a daze. Even the busiest streets, Broadway and Fifth Avenue, were empty of cars but full of wandering pedestrians. As we made our way downtown (I had already hooked up with a TV crew) we noticed small outdoor cafés open and people filling the sidewalk seats. People sat mostly in silence gazing upward at the thick plume of white smoke still snaking its way westward. At West Fourth Street, a group of kids played basketball. At one point the ball rolled out of play. A young shirtless boy ran after the ball and bent down to pick it up. When he lifted his head he looked up at the thick trail of smoke in the air. He shook his head and wiped away something from his eyes— either sweat or tears—and turned away.

I stopped and talked to a police officer. After chatting a few minutes, the officer asked me if I would like to see ground zero. I agreed to stay just at the edge, away from the workers.

The images on television of the devastation caused by Tuesday's attack do absolutely no justice to the scene of the crime. In real life it appears as if an asteroid had hit the lower part of Manhattan. There are charred, twisting slabs of metal and concrete in every direction. It is unfathomable and unspeakable. The tragedy today is in its infancy. For the thousands who lost their lives—parents, children, siblings, friends, and neighbors who walked out of their buildings one morning and have not returned—there are thousands more, friends and family, who will never sleep a restful night.

This is a national tragedy but also a very personal one. On Wednesday night while in a cab returning from work to my apartment, I noticed the Muslim name of my driver. He noticed the tone of my skin in the rear view mirror, and nodded at me. On the radio, the commentator was relaying a warning to all men of Middle Eastern and South Asian descent—to be wary of unwarranted violent reprisals from agitated residents of the city.

The taxi driver again looked at me in the mirror and smiled ironically. "We love America. It is our home." He shook his head. "But I think we're fucked."

❧

ABOUT A MONTH AGO, I rode up with two colleagues to the Northwest Frontier region of Pakistan bordering Afghanistan. We were covering a story on Islamic militancy training grounds based in Pakistani religious schools. In the West they have

widely been reported to be the training ground for the groom-
ing of young Muslim boys into hostile anti-Western terrorists.
In Pakistan, both the government and the men at the school
hotly contest these claims, castigating the West for generat-
ing such racist propaganda. I traveled to this lost area with
as little bias as possible—but with a certain and undeniable
fear in my heart.

In the school itself, the chancellor was most kind and hospitable. He invited us to tour the grounds of the school and
to meet teachers and some of the boys—though at first we
weren't allowed to talk to them. Then we were escorted into
his private residence.

The first thing I noticed on the center table was a bowl of
big yellow mangoes and a picture. The photograph was of our
host—a bearded older Muslim mullah wearing a traditional
white turban—and his friend Osama bin Laden, the man at
the top of the FBI's list of Most Wanted. I asked the mullah if
we could interview him. He agreed but insisted that first we
share mangoes. I agreed and he took out a long knife and pro-
ceeded to slice the fruit for me. We slurped and chatted for a
while and finally my crew was permitted to turn on the camera.

I asked the mullah a wide array of questions. Did he hate
the United States? Why is there such anti-Americanism in this
part of the world? Should Americans be afraid?

He answered them all eloquently and without hostility. He
talked about the history of the United States and Afghanistan,

how during the Cold War they were allies, united in fighting a war against the Soviets.

"You gave us weapons and trained our men. You built our roads, fed our people. Do you realize, young man, that your government helped to create and to fund the Taliban because it was their interest to use guerrilla warfare and terrorist tactics against the Russians? You made us your friend.

"But then your Cold War ended and you deserted us." At this point, a hint of animosity crept into his voice. "Because it was no longer in your selfish interest to have us as your allies, you abandoned us, left our people hungry, and hateful. You turned your friends into foes because you used us like whores."

There was a silence between us.

Finally I asked him about the picture, about the nature of his relationship with Mr. bin Laden.

"He's an old friend. And a good man."

I shook my head. "Is he a terrorist?"

"We don't call him that here."

The mullah made it clear he was not interested in talking anymore. We shook hands. I thanked him for his hospitality.

On the way out I thought about that hospitality. I knew that the mullah himself had endorsed a fatwa, or religious order, by bin Laden several years ago urging Muslims to kill American civilians. Yet here was this man cutting mangoes for us and being very gracious. It brought to mind an Afghan tradition: "Today you are our guest. If we were not hospitable, we would be very ashamed. But in times of war, yes you would be an enemy and we may kill you. Today a friend, tomorrow, *inshallah* (God willing), there will not be war."

❧

TODAY, FRIDAY, SEPTEMBER 14, 2001, four days since the terrorist attack, it appears we may be on the threshold of war. Our president has called it the first world war of the twenty-first century. I am not sure whom we will be fighting. I would like to visit my favorite café in the city, a small Egyptian place on the Lower East Side that I have been going to since college. The waiters—mostly young Middle Eastern guys who like to talk about basketball and soccer, who come and sit at your table and share a puff on the sweet tobacco hookas they serve there—are my friends. But I'm not sure when it will open again, if it will open again. There's a mosque next door that has been closed since the attack.

The weeks and months and perhaps even years ahead promise to be complex and wary. Hopefully our leaders will be judicious, precise, and compassionate in the difficult decisions that lie ahead. But it is each of us who now must rise up and be the true warriors in this difficult time. Does that mean seizing weapons and braving the threat of death out on a battlefield?

I think not. The battlefield is invisible. The enemy is elusive, and the web of evil too complex. Today there are no simple answers. It is too early for solutions.

For now we each have our stories—where we were on the day that the twin towers toppled. Each one is dramatic; each one is tragic. From this day forward, every day I shall observe a quiet remembrance for the victims of this calamity. We may each choose our own way to memorialize this moment, but I believe we are all obligated to reflect for a moment, to care about our neighbors, to meditate for peace and tolerance because ultimately the only forces that can defeat such profound evil are compassion and hope.

I hope you will find comfort and insight in the pages of this book. And I ask everyone to join my father and me in prayer for the healing of our wounded civilization (if we can call it that). Let us pray every day to whatever God we worship, remembering, as my dad has taught me since childhood, that Christ was not a Christian, Mohammed was not a Mohammedan, Buddha was not a Buddhist, and Krishna was not a Hindu.

—GOTHAM CHOPRA, *September 15, 2001*

PART I

In the Face of Tragedy

WHEN TERRORISTS FLEW two hijacked airliners into the World Trade Center towers, causing the deaths of more than 6,000 people, the immediate reaction was "life will never be the same again." The period of well-being our society had been enjoying ended. Our sense of security was replaced by fear. With one wrenching jolt, people awoke to the reality of collective suffering.

Three deaths out of the many weighed heavy on my heart. I never met Ruth Clifford McCourt, her four-year-old daughter Juliana, or Paige Farley Hackel. Ruth and Paige were best friends, and in photographs one sees them as particularly happy and loving women. On September 11, they were traveling together to California. They left home feeling lighthearted, because on this trip they would be surprising Juliana with a visit to Disneyland. Ruth and Paige split up at Logan Airport, each taking a separate flight in order to use frequent flyer miles. Paige boarded American Airlines flight 11. Ruth boarded United Airlines flight 175 with her daughter.

As fate would have it, both planes crashed into the twin towers, and all the passengers perished in a holocaust of ripped steel and burning jet fuel. With them died thousands of other innocent victims, who were granted only the slim mercy that unlike those on the airplanes, some in the buildings were caught by surprise and did not have to live under the certainty of their death sentence.

Every person can recall what it was like. So many of us watched the massive tragedy unfolding on television and some actually saw it in the sky. We felt inside our skin the death of hope that anyone would survive.

The media reported that at first the McCourt family, not knowing that Ruth and Juliana were on the doomed aircraft, thought they had been granted a miracle, because Ruth's brother, who worked in one of the towers, had escaped with his life. Only later were their spirits crushed by the terrible news of what had happened to Ruth and her child, Juliana.

Less widely reported was a fact that I knew personally. Ruth and Paige weren't just on vacation. They were coming to attend a course by Debbie Ford offered at the Chopra Center for Well Being in San Diego, intending to become healers. Death by violence is too tragic for irony, but the disparity between their spiritual goodness and their horrible fate was incredibly cruel. Ruth, Paige, and Juliana were three names on a list, yet they also became emblems of suffering, without choice or escape. The only fitting memorial that I could think of was to honor their memories by writing about the possibility of healing.

Stages of Suffering, Stages of Healing

❧

EVERYONE SUFFERS. In times of war or calamity or natural disasters, everyone suffers together. Yet no matter how far the dark ripples of pain might spread, suffering is always individual. We feel it inside as a wound to ourselves, but because it is invisible, we can't show this wound to anyone else. We can only live through the terrible experience of grief and depression, the sense of loss that overwhelms us so much that nothing else matters.

Suffering can be defined as the pain that makes life seem meaningless. Animals suffer, of course, and often deeply. Some are capable of mourning for their kind if one dies. Humans, however, are subject to complex inner pain that includes fear, guilt, shame, grief, rage, and hopelessness. It was an illusion to think that our society was immune to such suffering. That illusion abruptly burst on September 11.

On that day I was traveling cross-country when the airports were all shut down, forcing me to hire a rental car and to drive from city to city, mostly in the midwest between Detroit and Denver. As soon as I arrived anywhere, I met beseeching people who begged me to help them with their hurt and distress. In the first aftermath of a tragedy, victims experience numbness and shock. I was traveling during those first moments when shock was just giving way to tears, one of the very first stages of grief, so all anyone could do was to try to feel safe again on the most basic level. They might have read one of my books, heard a tape, or been to a workshop sometime in the past, and there I was, someone who might be able to help.

Yet I was in the same state they were in. All I could do was reflect on my own experiences with grief. "Hold each other," I offered. "Don't be afraid to ask for contact. Reach out and tell your loved ones that you do love them; don't let it be taken for granted. Feel your fear. Be with it and allow it to be released naturally. Pray. Grieve with others if you can, alone if you must."

These are simple, basic remedies for dealing with shock. But numbness and tears lead to the second stage, in which powerful emotions rise to the surface, often after being buried for years or decades. All around me I felt rage and sorrow starting to erupt. People began to say that they were deeply afraid in a way they had never experienced before. Now the most common incidents—the slam of a door, a car backfiring, a surprise tap on the shoulder—could trigger panic. In the ensuing days this anxiety began to spread like a contagion.

The third stage of suffering comes when you feel that you must take action, either to heal or to strike out against the attacker or to lend a hand to other victims. Many possibilities unfold. Some choices keep suffering going; others alleviate it. Before talking about the deep roots of suffering, we should pause over the choices that everyone can make when stage three begins.

Hold each other in loving awareness.

Speak gently.

Resist viewing negative images over and over.

Walk away when a conversation contains negativity.

*Keep your life as structured as possible—this is especially
true when dealing with children in the aftermath
of tragedy.*

*Try not to be alone—eat meals as a family, allow friends
to offer consolation, even when being around others
may be painful.*

*Forgive yourself when you feel like a victim, but take steps
to grow out of victim thinking.*

Allow for someone else's point of view. It is difficult to express inner pain, and we all do it imperfectly. What may seem like anger and frustration from others is often the best they can do.

Once the acute stages of grief have passed, your sense of suffering may be subtle, like a gray fog rather than a sharp physical wound. In this case, it is important to do more than strive to regain a sense of normalcy. The absence of acute suffering means that you are ready to start fulfilling your most fundamental needs once more, such as

The need for safety.
The need to belong.
The need to be acknowledged by others.
The need to matter.
The need to express yourself freely.
The need for love.

In their innocence, children will tell you outright what they need, but once we become adults, we learn to mask our emotions. I was amused and startled some years back when I saw a couple shopping with their little boy, who must have been around six. The parents were ignoring him, when suddenly the boy said in a loud voice, "You aren't loving me enough right now!" Mass tragedies are one of the few settings where the adult mask drops off. Disasters force people to cry in public, to exhibit fear that can't be hidden, to offer comfort because the need is so palpable.

On a practical level, nothing alleviates suffering like reaching out to another person who is suffering. Go and help, be of service if only in the smallest way. Each of us feels timid about reaching out to others; our society speaks of community but mostly we drift like atoms in a void. It isn't easy to reach over the walls built around our isolation, but any gesture—whatever you feel safe to do—is a step toward healing.

After the Pentagon and World Trade Center attacks, thousands of citizens from all walks of life volunteered to assist in search, rescue, support, and other efforts. Hundreds of thousands responded almost instantly to the call for blood donors. It would be impossible to single anyone out, but I was moved by one woman who rode her bicycle down to the disaster site in order to find her niece and nephew, which, miraculously, she did. The next day, she was drawn again to the site—as so many people said they were—by an invisible force. She found a few other women who also felt the call to help, so they started making sandwiches for the rescue teams, at first a few at a time, but these quickly grew to be hundreds. Within a few days she was managing entire truck deliveries of meals and leading dozens of volunteers.

"I had an extraordinary experience, one that I hope won't be misunderstood," she later said. "This turned into the best five days of my life." The reason tragedy turned to light for her was that she made a heart connection with others; a human thread now linked her to the life we all share. It is this connection we crave the most. But it is up to us to find the will to weave the first strand.

Even though your ego may cry out as if only you are in pain, you need to look further. Offering help to others ends your isolation, a primary source of your pain. A woman stood up at a lecture once and asked me, "How can I get rid of this terrible pain in my heart? It has been with me for twenty years, ever since I lost a child." I had given specific answers to similar questions, but this time I blurted out, "You have to stop thinking of it as *your* pain." I expected her to look shocked or offended. What crossed her face instead was a puzzled look, as if she knew that something true had been hinted at. My pain? Of course it's mine. Who else could it belong to?

What if the pain that seems to be yours is really not yours? (And here I do not mean to belittle personal suffering, but only to offer a larger perspective that may help alleviate it.) The truth is that fear and anger exist outside ourselves. They are not yours or mine, unless we attract them. Negativity is an invisible parasite. It needs a host to feed off of, and the host is the ego. When you learned as a young child to cling to *my* toy, *my* candy, *my* pleasure, *my* happiness, at the same time your ego started clinging to the opposite: *my* scraped knee, *my* broken doll, *my* sadness, *my* pain. Absorbing an experience as "mine" was how you built your self up, developed a sense of individual identity. As we grew, we learned to see this self in a larger perspective, in the context of humanity. But when tragedy strikes, we often regress to this early state.

To counteract this, we need to find the spirit. For spirit can do one thing that your ego craves very deeply and can't accomplish on its own. Spirit can help the ego escape that painful trap of I, me, and mine. It is strange but true that the very mechanism that builds the isolated self also wants to escape it. The ego wants the best for "me," yet there is another, subtler force that wants the best for all (which ends up being best for me, in the end). Allow this force to express itself, and you will discover that the walls of isolation are not as solid as your suffering makes them seem.

I felt tears come to my eyes just after the collapse of the World Trade Center's twin towers, when one TV reporter was interviewing a woman who had just run out of that billowing, choking dust that filled the air. He was trying to do a professional job, and she was doing her best to uphold her end. "Describe the scene you've just left," the reporter said. He held the microphone under her face, and the woman searched for a good answer, when all at once her expression crumpled, and she began to cry. The reporter didn't say, "Cut the camera" or "Go ahead and take a moment." Quicker than words he put his arm around her, and before the gaze of the world she cried and cried. He let her do this for as long as she wanted, and I cried, too.

Spirit gives us access to an emotion that cannot be felt in isolation—compassion. Compassion comes from the root words "to suffer with," and for that reason many people actually fear it. An audience member in Boston on a gray drizzly evening asked me, "How can I feel compassion for the victims of this tragedy without having it hurt me? I don't want to be injured, I want to offer love and peace." It was a very honest question, and I responded, I hope, on that level.

"Let yourself feel their pain. Let it come into you, and don't be afraid that you'll be injured. Trying to keep out someone else's pain comes from fear for our own safety; in the name of safety we retreat behind our own private walls. Yet the truth is that your pain and the pain of the victims are shared. They make you human together."

Compassion is one of the most honored and saintly feelings because it marches up to the front lines of suffering and says, "Take me." In this giving of oneself there is a direct experience of pain, yet in the giving there is love. Thus compassion has the power to dissolve pain by not avoiding it, but by trusting that love affords the greatest protection. By discovering that there is a reality—love—stronger than any pain, you mount your strongest defense.

The Anatomy of Fear

THE VICTIMS AT ground zero on September 11 suffered most, but we all suffered in kind. We felt the icy grip of fear, even if our own physical danger had not in fact significantly increased. Uncertainty and insecurity became common sensations, and for many they will not go away, not completely at least. In the natural grieving process, layers of fear and suffering come to the surface. If this process is denied or cut short, the trauma turns into a deep and lasting wound. Yet because it hurts to grieve, everyone is tempted to skip this stage; there is resistance.

"We were all lulled in the nineties," one younger person said after the terrorist attacks. "We lived inside a protected bubble. As long as the bubble lasted, no one would get hurt. Prosperity was endless, happiness awaited in the future. I knew that it felt unreal, but I never expected the bubble to be pierced from the outside. Now no one seems to know what to do." In the face of tragedy the easy emotion is anger. Like all feelings, anger should not be denied, but it will not substitute for releasing deeper, more difficult wounding.

Healing takes courage. When we were small children, there was a wide gap between what we feared and what was real, even if we didn't realize it at the time. In the middle of the night our parents could comfort us after bad dreams, reassure us that the bogeyman didn't exist, protect us from the phantoms conjured up in our minds.

Adults seek the same protection, but for us it is sometimes much harder to close the gap between fear and reality. When the government reacted to the World Trade Center attack, as well as the attack on Washington and the hijacking that ended in a crash in Pennsylvania, by vowing revenge on terrorism around the world, the patriarchs in our society were trying to be good parents and protectors. Yet our enemies, they said, were invisible and hiding in shadows. No one really knew who they were, and after a while it was easy to imagine them everywhere. So protection was denied us at the very moment we needed it most. In the ensuing days the stock market fell. Although planes were flying again, I walked through airports hearing rumblings on all sides about the collapse of the economy. Confidence was ebbing rapidly.

Because I am writing this a week after the tragedy, I don't know how that sense of doom has played out. One has the sense at this time that it might get worse long before it gets better. Freud said that no emotion is more unwelcome than anxiety. It arrives and refuses to leave. In the face of terror, thinking shuts down. The body's defense systems scream out warnings, and the grip of fear takes hold. The physical sensation of fear is actually our ally in times of crisis, because it triggers the hormonal system into the fight-or-flight response. We don't know how our ancestors responded to threat psychologically, but we can be certain that their bodies were equipped to fight back or to flee from danger.

Fear takes a downward spiral when threats won't go away, as we see in a home where children can't escape from abuse. But it is most visibly experienced, perhaps, during war. "I went to Sarajevo as part of a mercy mission in the mid-nineties," a man told me recently. "The scene was horrendous. Snipers fired from buildings. Artillery shelling was an everyday occurrence. People walked around knowing that they could die while buying a piece of fruit at the open market or simply walking from a parking lot into work.

"As a visitor to this manmade hell, I felt the fear that never leaves you. When you are eating dinner or catching a cup of coffee at a café, normal life is just a thin screen. What you sensed all the time was fear, the underlying reality. My heart found a reason to pound at least ten times a day, and getting to sleep at night was nearly impossible unless you exhausted yourself to the point where your body had no other option."

Reports from war zones testify to all of these feelings. But even though outward events create the setting for fear, people can experience anxious situations quite differently from each other. The man continued, "The population of Sarajevo had been suffering much longer and more intensely than I, as a visitor, ever could. It was curious how some could manage to be almost cheerful and normal, while others were sunk in a deep lethargy, like half-awake sleepwalkers. The men in particular channeled their fear into anger. You heard talk of the enemy and retaliation everywhere you went, and if you tried to bring up the truth that violence begets violence, you risked getting beaten up.

"The women, on the other hand, were sunk into a sorrowful kind of helplessness. You don't realize the lively, light quality that women bring into everyday existence until it goes missing. In Sarajevo nothing was light and lively. I almost felt that no innocent young girls would ever be born again. There would just be one unending grayness forever."

I'd like to discuss each of these symptoms in the anatomy of fear separately, because healing differs depending on what stage of anxiety a person is in and on individual reactions to that fear.

Shock and numbness: The mind is used to protecting itself

from threats by overlooking and denying them. Even though something very bad might be easily predictable—heart disease in a person who never exercises, smokes, and eats a high-fat diet —the news that you have a potentially fatal condition arrives with a shock. If your mind has lulled itself successfully enough, a huge amount of distress that has long been stuffed away now erupts all at once. This stress is too much to absorb. By numbing itself, your mind is able to dam the flood for a while.

In the natural course of time, shock and numbness end. As mentioned above, this is just the first stage. The pent-up energies of anger, fear, and grief want to find a way out. Yet a person can curtail their natural flow, remaining numb by choice. One can decide at some level that resistance is the only way to survive. As a result the person's inner world becomes constricted. Since none of us can say that we have freed ourselves completely from the traumas of the past, psychiatrists uncover huge reservoirs of pain in people who thought that their only problem was insomnia or the inability to hold on to a relationship. The issue of numbness is much bigger than we realize.

Constricted awareness robs you of freedom in many ways. It is like an invisible vise, tightening down your emotional response, squeezing your vital potential to the bare minimum. Although it sounds abstract, constricted awareness causes a vast array of problems. They begin with insensitivity: when you are forcing yourself not to feel, you cannot be sensitive to others. You cannot empathize with their situation; you are not open to another's point of view. Insensitive people appear aloof and cut off. They seem not to care about anyone else's feelings, when in reality they are unable to. Their constricted awareness is totally focused on handling their own distress, conscious or unconscious.

Helplessness and vulnerability: For most of us, after the initial shock wears off, the mind tries to raise its old defenses, but often they don't work anymore. The impact of stress is too great; the emotions welling up refuse to be pushed down again. When you find that you have no defense against your own fear, you begin to feel vulnerable. In many ways it is healthy to feel vulnerable. It shows that you are not cut off, either from yourself or others. But the feeling of helplessness is extremely difficult to live with. This alone can raise dread, and the mind struggles to regain control.

Panic: The next stage, if you are unable to regain a sense of control, is panic. Panic arises when the mind is so overloaded by distress that all coherence is lost. Fear roams the mind at will, breaking down every barrier. Because the mind-body system is arranged to restore balance by any means, this total incoherence lasts for only a short time. Panic is one of the most frightening experiences anyone can have, but it is almost always temporary.

Panic attacks, which strike some people without any external cause, depend upon memory of past trauma, as do all anxiety attacks. Images generated inside the mind become triggers, as if they were external events, and the chain reaction of fear follows of its own accord. Because old images can revisit to cause harm long after they are viewed, it is vitally important to protect young children from seeing the kind of terrifying pictures that the media broadcasts during catastrophes. Children who seem to have no fearful response to events like those of September 11 are often postponing their reactions until much later. Those of us who grew up during the Cold War can attest to the horror we felt for many years after seeing photos of atom-bomb testing, yet I never remember showing any of this inner dread to my parents. It was private, and especially frightening for that reason.

However acute, panic isn't the measure of how extreme a crisis is externally. When jets are about to crash—and this happened on the doomed planes involved in the terrorist attack as well as inside the twin towers—people become quiet and turn to tell one another that they love them. Such calm often leads to acts of bravery: from cell phone conversations that were held from the jetliner that crashed in Pennsylvania, we know that on at least one plane, the passengers resisted the terrorists even though they knew with certainty that they would die.

Anger: Anger can be a primary emotion, but in the world of fear it is a secondary defense. People become enraged when they are unable to overcome their feelings of helplessness. Lashing out serves two purposes. It makes you feel that you are in control again, and without control some people would be in complete panic. Second, it directs emotions outward, giving a visible external enemy to attack.

You have to become aware of your primary emotion before you can release it. If you know your primary emotion is helplessness—in the terrorist attacks this was easy to admit—anger can be managed and seen for what it is, a defense. If you refuse to accept that you could ever lose control and become helpless, anger justifies itself as the "right" response. From there it is a short journey to intolerance and violence.

Anxiety: Chronic fear, the kind that wakes you up in the night and strikes without warning in everyday life, is termed anxiety. It is one of the most prevalent forms of suffering in our society, magnified after the terrorist attacks yet present long before. Anxiety feels like unnamed dread. It can be managed medically, though tranquilizers are not the same as a cure. It can be felt in milder degrees, making the person constantly nervous and on edge, or it can be felt acutely, when a person is flooded with terror for no apparent reason.

Fear becomes anxiety when a threat loses its immediate edge but cannot be forgotten. Anxiety is based on memory. It comes not from outside but from our inner world. Because it grows out of primitive responses to physical danger, anxiety remains linked to outer events. A woman who is told that the lump in her breast is malignant will plunge into anxiety, and until she becomes healthy again, her anxiety may continue.

Depression: Although it may not show, depression contains

an underlying component of fear and anxiety. Depression is pain directed against the self. Looking at depressed people's facial expressions, you immediately read how dull, withdrawn, exhausted, and sad they feel. Their approach to life is passive and resigned. We tend to forget this and treat depression as a weakness, particularly our own; if others can find joy in life, then it's our fault that we have failed to. Such judgments get connected to guilt, and depressed people are often acutely aware of letting down family and friends. They see themselves as the gray cloud threatening every happy occasion.

If you look at depression without judgment, it can be seen as the final battlefront against fear. Depressed people are on the verge of giving up, and indeed some will make the perilous choice of trying to end their lives. But before that stage, depression is a last line of defense, in which the mind runs for cover, shutting all operations down to a minimum, providing just enough life support for survival. Although it has become so commonplace that the word "depression" falls from our lips carelessly, as though we were discussing the flu or a bad headache, I can't escape its deep pathos. To me, seeing a depressed person is like watching a magnificent racehorse that has broken its leg. So much magnificence is possible for a human being that to see it shut down and almost extinguished is heartbreaking.

So what is the best way to deal with the many guises of fear? No matter what stage a person may be in, fear can be released. One starts by reaching out and beginning to talk, freely and expressively, about feeling afraid. If this seems impossible because you have been taught that fear is a sign of weakness, talk about that. Guilt is a tremendous obstacle in this regard, and so is shame. But an opening must be found, and I believe the following steps are effective:

Be with your fear, seeing it as a bodily sensation.
Think of this sensation as rooted in old energies that have
*   been stored up.*
Ask that pent-up energy to flow out of your body.
Assist this flow until you have released what is ready to
*   leave right now.*

Each step has its own technique. First, feeling fear as a bodily sensation gets it out of the realm of the mind. Fear has a voice. It speaks of many dangers; it accumulates scenarios of doom and whirls from one to the other without end. As a voice, fear is extremely persuasive, yet the words are connected to bodily reactions. These are much easier to release than your thoughts. Thoughts come and go, often increasing in intensity the more you resist them. Bodily sensations are more objective.

First locate your bodily sensations of fear. These often include tightened muscles—first explore the susceptible areas of neck, forehead, chest, pit of the stomach, and lower back. Sometimes we feel pronounced weakness or heaviness in the limbs. Whenever your thoughts are racing, it is likely that your blood pressure may be rising, but there is no way to physically feel this. You want a sensation you can locate. Concentrate on your racing pulse, butterflies in your stomach, weak knees and rubbery legs, and so forth—whatever you associate with fear or anxiety in any form.

These sensations are the biological residue of experience. When you recall being frightened by something, for example, your body revisits the scene as surely as your mind, and instead of merely remembering, it re-creates the same symptoms you felt at the moment. The same cold stab of fear comes back, carrying with it a particular bodily signature, which is the expression of its energy. In healing, the energy is more important than the accompanying thoughts. Like a pebble in your shoe, a disturbing energy reminds you of its presence by sending out signals of pain. It does no good to keep thinking about how much the pebble hurts; until you remove the source of the energy, no healing has occurred. Similarly, fear and anxiety send up countless thoughts, but until you move the energy, attending to the thoughts will not bring lasting relief. Fear will just attach itself to a new set of thoughts.

Now ask for this unwanted energy to leave, and assist it to depart. This assistance, the most critical step, can be done in many ways.

Deep, relaxed breathing. Reach down to your lower abdomen with each inhalation, then let the air whoosh out naturally, the way you would release a sigh.

Listening. Ask inside what the energy wants you to know. We all have thousands of pockets of remembered trauma, each with their own story. Freely open yourself to hearing and seeing where the energy is coming from. As you receive the messages and images, your fear will be met with understanding, making it more susceptible to release.

Move. Trapped energies are frozen; they are like ice jams in the river of awareness or plaque built up in arteries. What is stuck needs to be turned into motion. Freezing needs to thaw. For many people it helps to move physically. Running and moving about is a good release for superficial tension. The deeper energies respond if you physically act them— writhing, shaking, and trembling, for example, if they reflect what you feel. Stomping and flailing are effective when the stuck energy is rooted in anger.

Make sounds. Anguish has an inarticulate voice, a voice that doesn't like words because they are too weak for the intensity of feeling that is present. Anguish prefers to scream. It shouts, moans, groans, whimpers, and chokes with sobbing. As you feel the deep sensations of your fear, allow such sounds to emerge naturally. Don't force them. (Screaming into a pillow can be a tremendous help.)

Start more gently by toning. When you feel a bodily sensation, hum or coo the tone of that sensation, then let the energy carry the tone, high or low, anywhere it wants to go. If toning seems foreign, begin with that satisfied "Hmm" that comes spontaneously at the thought of something delicious to eat. That is a tone (and you already let out many others, such as moaning sighs, groans of disappointment, guttural grunts with physical effort). You may have shied away from tones of grief, its high wailing, or from a baby's sobs, which wrench its whole body, but they are still available to you. So is the shriek that is one's first response to a shocking blow, particularly if it comes as a surprise. All of these belong in your arsenal against fear, and since they directly involve your body as well as the emotional centers in the brain, tones have a powerful ability to locate distress, express it, and then carry it away.

THERE IS ANOTHER crucial element to releasing fear. I have observed that we are all willing to release our most intimate and hidden fears when we feel trust. Trust means that you are offered the promise of safety and can accept it. Both parts are necessary—there has to be the offer of emotional openness and also the ability to accept that a safe haven is truly present.

The question is, where can any of us turn for trust? First you must trust yourself, finding enough security so you are not blocked from your own release. We all feel inhibited. It is embarrassing to cry out in anguish. Look inside and ask yourself if you hold any of the following beliefs:

I've been hurting so long that it's too late to change.
I'm waiting for someone to notice my pain.
My pain means that I am alive.
I deserve to be this way.
Why won't someone rescue me?
I am crying out to be loved.
I am not meant to understand.

Each of these attitudes gives you a reason to prolong suffering and block its release. Every time you repeat these rationales, you thicken the walls that imprison you. You have the choice to hold on to these beliefs for as long as you want, but trapped energies become stronger the more they are repressed. The cycle of denial and suffering has to be broken. In place of the negative beliefs that have thickened the walls of repression, begin to absorb those beliefs that make the walls thinner, even if you haven't fully accepted them yet. Each positive belief reverses a negative one.

It doesn't matter how long I've been hurting this way;
>   *I can change.*
Perhaps not enough people have noticed my pain and taken
>   *it seriously, but I have noticed, and that is enough.*
My pain doesn't make me alive, it shuts out countless
>   *possibilities by blocking them from my life.*

I deserve to be healed.

I don't need rescuing; I need help. There is always someone
willing to help.

I am desperate to be loved, so it is time to find the right
person, someone who can hear my words and respond
to my need.

I may not understand what is happening to me now, but
if I undertake the healing journey, understanding
will come.

What you are developing is a healing attitude. You can
launch out in many directions from here. Keep this list of
beliefs close at hand, and when you feel discouraged, go back
to it. Discuss with others how they have transformed a negative attitude into a positive one. Take a single item from the
negative list and devote an entire day to examining how that
belief has affected you, then take the next day to supply a
positive belief in its place. Keep a journal in which you honestly divulge to yourself the ways in which negative beliefs
influence you, as well as positive beliefs. Developing a new
belief system is a campaign, and you must wage the battle
from two directions.

If reading the negative statements arouses anger or other
resistance, pay special attention; you have touched a nerve.
If you truly feel that you can't change, being told that you

can will arouse frustration, rage, self-pity, defeatism—a host of stepchildren who follow in the wake of hopeless resignation. Bring these feelings forward. Write them down. Sit at your computer and title a page, "Why I Will Never Change" or "Why No One Sees That I Am in Pain." Let fly all your certainty that you have been victimized and hurt, neglected and overlooked. Don't edit or judge your thoughts as you write them. Until you face how you feel—not what you should feel—healing can't begin.

At a certain point you will turn the corner and become excited about bringing a new, positive belief system into reality.

At whatever stage of this journey you find yourself, the same reminders apply every day—don't force anything. Appreciate every tiny insight, every meager opening. It seems like a small thing to remove one brick at a time, until the day the whole prison collapses.

Be patient and gentle with yourself. Don't get sidetracked by anger. Once you know what has made you angry and frustrated, stop venting. Ask for answers to your frustration; consciously reach for the deeper source, which is always fear. Working through the entire labyrinth of anxiety or depression may take years, but if you are determined, healing takes much less time than it took to build up the wounds, and relief from anxiety can come quickly. You will experience a large measure of healing from the act of beginning this process.

Fear can be dispelled, even when it runs extremely deep, but fear must be respected until you find a way to release it. Ask yourself how much fear, distress, and anxiety your parents felt comfortable talking to you about. (I am referring to their own pain, not the pain you brought to them when you felt troubled, although that too will give you some indications.) If you recall that your father hid any trace of anxiety, even when money was tight or his job was in jeopardy or serious illness threatened, you have demarked a boundary that you may feel reluctant to cross today, now that you are an adult. If your mother suffered in silence or passively accepted that anxious situations could not be dealt with, again you have demarked a boundary that you may have internalized as a child.

Emotional boundaries are passed on from one generation to the next. Therapists can spend years with some patients before they will open up. Respect your defenses even while working to dissolve them. Inner walls don't come crashing down; they melt. So don't think anyone expects you to bravely assault your defenses and plunge through them like a warrior. Your greatest weapons are willingness, honesty, and patience.

Having made a space for trusting yourself, now you need someone else to trust. Healing is not a matter of solitary work. Don't automatically put your best friend, spouse, or big sister at the top of your list. Be objective about who is emotionally available and who isn't. Look for someone who is tolerant and accepting of their own flaws, someone who listens well and doesn't impose their own judgments on others. These are people you can begin to trust. Approach such a person and ask permission to share one kind of distress that you really want to talk about. Sharing is crucial, for if you expect them to be open to you, it is only fair that you be open to them. However, it is entirely justified that you ask for a privileged time when the talk will be solely about you if you are feeling acute distress. The implied bargain is that when they feel their own distress, you will be available. Be sensitive to when you have gone too far and are just using another person's sympathetic ear as a dumping zone. Don't ask for advice. The best use of sympathy is to find someone whom you trust enough to begin the process of release that you must continue on your own. Your intention is to bring shy, hidden, embarrassing, guilty, or shameful energies into view. This exposure sets the stage for dealing with these energies.

Do we all personally have such a person in our lives? No, not by a long shot. Two things can be said about this. First, you can seek out professional help and ease into deep trust, moving at your own speed and sensing—not from the mind but from the heart—if he or she is truly open enough to accept the darker energies you want to release. Second, there is a spiritual law that I have been able to trust completely over the years: When you are ready, guidance will come. Rely

on the people who are in your life now; face your dark energies as honestly as you can; respect your boundaries and
those of everyone around you. As you peel back each layer
of the onion, the teacher who can lead you on will show
up, almost miraculously matching the very moment when
guidance is needed.

"Why? Tell Me Why."

THINK OF THE LAST TIME you were called on to comfort someone in crisis. Over and over I'm sure they asked one question:
Why? Our minds can't accept random, meaningless pain. One
commentator on the catastrophe in New York remarked in its
aftermath, "Only a week has passed, but walking down the
street I see the panhandlers out again on Broadway and the
guys passing out leaflets for lap dancing in front of Penn Station. Rescue workers are still using their bare hands to dig
through steel and rubble, but life has come back anyway, because people want meaning to come back. The meaning isn't in
the facts of the tragedy. We need to find out the facts, certainly,
yet they cannot make this catastrophe have any meaning."

The same quandary haunts every victim of crime, disease,
injustice, and loss. Why did this happen to me? What did I do

to deserve it? If there is a God, how can He allow such suffering to exist? In the search for meaning, three large answers have emerged. You find them in every culture.

THE FIRST ANSWER: *Suffering is inevitable because it is part of life.*

THE SECOND ANSWER: *Suffering is unnatural, the result of sin and wrongdoing.*

THE THIRD ANSWER: *Suffering contains a hidden spiritual message. It exists until the message is heard.*

The first answer—suffering is an inevitable part of life—is based on nature. Every creature is born and dies. In between these two poles, creatures fight to remain alive. The physical body is exposed to danger from every side—famine, violence, accidents, aging, and death are the most prominent. If you dig up the remains of prehistoric humans, their bodies are ravaged by almost all of these threats. Therefore it seems only natural that you and I must suffer, because nature is simply designed that way for all animals. Let's call this the fatalistic view, because although human beings have fought for centuries to alleviate famine and disease, other causes of suffering, such as war and violence, have proved incurable. After the horrendous events of September 11, I could sense in myself and all those around me the voice of fatalism saying, "Try as hard as you want, but in the end you will never rid human nature of irrational violence and hatred." This voice arises from the first answer, that suffering is inevitable.

The second answer—suffering is unnatural, growing out of sin and wrongdoing—states the exact opposite. Instead of considering all the natural forces that threaten us, it declares that humans suffer from the inside out, not from the outside in. Our choices to follow wrong action come back to haunt us. Humans are the only creatures wracked by guilt and shame. We feel pain when we commit a sin like murder, whereas animals show no remorse when they exhibit violence. Sin-based suffering is far more terrible than mere physical pain. It gives birth to anxiety and depression, which are mysterious afflictions, since these two ghosts of the mind haunt people even when they have done nothing wrong. Just the perception of doing wrong can create intense guilt. But any creature that can commit a sin must be capable of doing the right thing. Therefore the second answer is actually optimistic. Despite the evidence of centuries past, we dream of redemption. Every religion wants to end suffering by taking humans back to some state of innocence or ahead to some paradise. Therefore we can call the second answer idealistic. If I look inside myself during those moments of shock after September 11, I hear a voice saying, "Keep trying, you are better than this terrible act of evil. Your spirit can rise above it." This voice comes from the second answer, that suffering is unnatural.

The third answer—suffering contains a hidden spiritual

message—is very different from the other two. It says that out of suffering can come love. Love is the hidden message within all fear and pain, no matter how horrible they make you feel. The idea that suffering contains a spiritual message goes beyond fatalism and idealism both, because the distinction between inner and outer, physical and mental is erased. Instead, we are seen as pure spirit, which has chosen to walk on the stage of the natural world in order to play out soul dramas. Sometimes the drama is happy and joyful; sometimes the drama is painful and full of sorrow. Spirit is above any drama. It is the sweet, unheard music of life itself. During the World Trade Center and Pentagon catastrophes, I believe a silent voice was reaching through the pain to say, "You feel hurt and afraid, but you are not your feelings. You experience tragedy, but you remain untouched by it. You see the face of death, but behind that mask there is eternal love." This voice arises from the third answer, that suffering contains a hidden spiritual message; that message is always love. Terrorists don't care about themselves, and they are convinced they can do anything because they burn with hatred. If you didn't care about yourself yet burned with love instead, you could help save the world.

There are many ways to relieve pain, but I believe that only spirituality can heal suffering. To hope for an end to suffering is idealistic, and even though Buddha, Christ, Mohammed, and other great spiritual teachers have offered a vision where suffering ends, it is also true that suffering ennobles people, teaches us lessons, guides us toward insight, and purifies our nature. Suffering is a paradox.

ॐ

FINALLY, WE CAN put our trust in the following principles:

ॐ Fear is powerful, but your soul is unafraid. Find your soul and it will dissolve your suffering.

At any moment you are asked either to believe in the reality presented by your fear or the reality presented by your soul. Fear speaks from the ego, the limited "I." Ego has a lot to accomplish in the world, and you rely on it to build yourself up, to acquire things, to assert the needs of "me" versus "them." A core teaching of Buddhism holds that ego itself is the root cause of suffering. But in normal life we must all live with ego and its needs; we have grown totally accustomed to seeing the world from an individual point of view. So I prefer to perceive its reality as an early stage of self-development.

ॐ When you have lived long enough the way ego tells you to, another reality presents itself. This is the soul's reality.

The first tenet of the soul's reality is that you are more than mind and body.

The second tenet is that you are never alone.

The third is that compassion enables you to feel equality with all living things. When awareness is fully expanded, you have arrived at the soul—not my soul, but the essence and source of spirit in everyone.

The Meaning of Death

THE BRUTE FACT of death is nearly impossible to face. No one denies that we all must die, yet we go on living without admitting that death is stalking us, drawing nearer with each breath. This defense supposedly is created by the conscious mind to avoid the terrors of the unconscious. If so, that defense broke down completely on September 11, when death exploded into a sunny day for all to see. One man standing blocks away from the World Trade Center observed what he thought were specks of falling debris. Then he raised a pair of binoculars to his eyes and saw that the debris was flailing the air as it fell. He turned his face away with horror and prayed that he might forget what he saw. It is unacceptable to find more grief in one death than another, but perhaps these suicides were the most pitiable that day.

"I saw workers leaping out of the windows," an eyewitness recalled who was in the second tower after the first was hit. "They were jumping because their offices had filled with burning jet fuel. The heat of the fireball was over a thousand degrees Fahrenheit. You could see the neckties on the men pointing upward as they fell. Two people held hands on the way down—perhaps they were friends or perhaps husband and wife. The last token of their love was to die together. A few didn't jump or fall to their deaths but spread their arms and dived headfirst. More than anything, I felt the heartbreak of that kind of brave and gallant gesture." Another person, a parent whose children viewed the tragedy from their school, said that his kids came home and told him what color of clothing the suicides were wearing, so close did they see it all. On the ground, one firefighter was killed instantly when a man falling from the towers landed on him.

Dying is horrifying to us on many levels. It is a fearful prospect to suffer intense physical pain, and since we have all felt it, our minds recoil from experiencing more. The prospect of being annihilated, of disappearing into the void as experience comes to an end, creates perhaps the deepest fear. In response, people try to escape awareness of mortality in all the ways we've become familiar with, from substance abuse to our culture's endless fascination with youth and beauty.

Death as a fact becomes less brutal if you can accept that it is a necessary part of life. The universe recycles everything in the never-ending flow of time. The atoms that make up your body have found a temporary shelter only. Like birds of passage they are always in flight. With your next breath you will take in several billion molecules of air once breathed by Buddha or Jesus, and when you exhale you will send molecules of air to be breathed tomorrow by people in China. Every other atom of your body is borrowed and must be repaid to the cosmos. The reason that the ancient Indians worshiped Shiva, the god of death and dissolution, wasn't out of fear alone, or a desire to placate him. The traditions of wisdom looked at nature and saw in its design creation and dissolution, the one inseparable from the other. At the deepest level, everyone is borrowing and repaying all the time. The scene isn't one of perpetual death but of life circulating within itself.

Recently several dozen people were gathered in a small room where I was leading a meditation. It seemed like a good idea to let them hear for themselves how the heart slows down when you put your attention on it in silence. This heart meditation is very powerful, and I wanted to prove that to them with physical evidence. Anyone who has run on a treadmill at the gym has probably seen those chest belts that you fasten on as you run; the device monitors your heartbeat and gives readout on a small device like a beeper attached to your wrist. When the audience was outfitted with their chest belts, I asked them to close their eyes. Soft, soothing music was put on, but before I could begin the guided meditation, one person noticed that she was having pressure in her chest. Immediately another complained of pounding in his chest. Then two people reported palpitations. Startled, I asked them to remove the chest belts—I was afraid these people had cardiac problems. But the next day, when the maker of the chest belts was contacted, he said, "Oh, didn't I tell you? In a small room there's a lot of cross talk among the devices."

What he meant was that the monitors, by amplifying one person's heartbeat, send a signal that the next person's heart can hear. In fact every heart in the room was talking—and listening—to every other. What an extraordinary thing! Then I realized that this cross talk goes on constantly. The monitors were only exaggerating a kind of heart-to-heart connection we all have with each other all the time.

This wasn't the end of it. The next day I was standing on the roof of the Chopra Center getting a breath of fresh air when I sensed that someone nearby was smoking. This didn't seem possible—I was alone three stories up. My eye caught a man smoking a cigarette two blocks away, and I realized it was he. It was a vivid demonstration that we literally share each other's every breath, for the cigarette smoke was just a tracer. I was inhaling oxygen and carbon, nitrogen and hydrogen, that just a few seconds before had been circulating in this stranger's body. In essence he was sharing his body with me, and with everyone else on earth.

When you realize how intimately connected we all are, the reality that life is a common possession, more like an eco-system than like a new car, hits home. Like my heart and my breathing, my mind is recirculating images and feelings that are shared with millions of other people. Without death, this renewal would not be possible.

At another level such arguments carry little weight, be-cause they are not addressed to one's deep, almost physical fear of death. In the East it is believed that our bodies store the memories of many deaths as we move from one incarnation to the next. Thus our terror at the prospect of dying is really a memory. Likewise, the peace that can be felt in the face of death is also a memory. Each of us is susceptible to both recollections, the pain of dying and the joy of being reborn. Without having to endorse any belief in reincarnation, I have found that people do locate the memory of peace inside. In fact Elisabeth Kübler-Ross's now-famous six stages of dying are a journey from resistance, fear, and denial to that point of inner peace that accepts that death is not to be feared.

Since the fear of death exists on many levels, so does its healing. On the emotional level you need to begin ridding yourself of the energy of fear—we have already covered how that is done. On the mental level you can read philosophy or scriptures, or if you are a nonbeliever, delve into the many sci-entific studies of near-death experiences, which have now been documented by the thousands. Faith can come in through the mind. Much of my own faith has come from reading the Bible, the Vedas, the poetry of Tagore and Rumi, writings from modern spiritual teachers in every culture, as well as from scientific essays.

It gives comfort to read in the Upanishads that our lives are like ripples in the vast ocean of consciousness; like waves we rise and fall, yet we never disappear, for the ocean is infinite and eternal, and a wave is nothing but that ocean. It is equally comforting to read the scientific equivalent of the same statement, which holds that everything in existence is a wave of energy, and even though the wave function may collapse to form an electron whose life is finite, the field that gives rise to energy remains infinite, eternal, unmoving, and undying. The same words that apply to God also apply to any description of the ultimate reality. The mind is a great healer once you give it enough information and many points of view to absorb.

Yet wherever you place your faith, death remains mysterious. Many times I have felt that a talk I've just given on the meaning of death has brought solace to an audience, yet without fail someone stands up and says, "But we don't really know what happens, do we? I'm still afraid I'm going to die and turn into nothing." No one fully accepts the reassurances being offered by reason or religion.

"I thought I was getting over my fear of death," one middle-aged woman told me, "until I had to witness my dear grandmother dying last year. The final stages took twelve hours, and when she became aware of her surroundings at the end, all I saw in her eyes was fear and panic. She loved and cared for me so much—I could hardly stand this being so traumatic for her. Please help me, I'm haunted by her eyes."

Dying is a natural process, but our attitudes toward it can be very unnatural. The fear of death witnessed here is rooted in deep emotional clinging. Whatever you resist you will fear. When people are dying, they often try to make it go away by saying, "This isn't happening to me, it can't be true. Something will save me." As the dying process continues, resistance makes it more and more painful.

But of course you can be just as afraid of dying before it happens—the fear itself is what needs to be healed. In every wisdom tradition there is a teaching called "dying unto death," as the New Testament calls it. This means experiencing the truth about dying while you are still alive. At this moment your body could not be alive without death. Billions of cells have to perish to bring new ones to life. You could not think or feel or dream if your mind did not allow your old thoughts to die away and make room for the new.

So it is a myth to think that death is "out there" waiting for us. Death is here with us, tied into the flow of life. There is a wonderful saying, "You will never be more alive than you are at this moment, and you will never be more dead than you are this moment." Your goal, then, should be to experience yourself as fully as you can, to become so alive that death will no longer be a threat. Don't see yourself as struggling to remain alive against all obstacles; see yourself as a river that accepts all change because change is natural as you move from one life stage to the next. When asked why he was so calm about dying, Socrates said, "I've been walking toward this destination all my life. Why should the last footstep make me afraid?"

Yet how should we feel when we think that we, or a person we love, could disappear and not come back again? You can bring fear or peace to this thought; the choice is yours. We would all want to bring peace, and to do that you have to experience through meditation and prayer the deep, still, quiet within yourself. Having found that, you will never be surprised by death. For to die is to return to this same silence, this pure awareness known as "the light." When people say after a near-death experience that they went into the light, they are reporting on a destination that is always with us. The light is your pure being.

Here is another image. Imagine that inside you is a space nothing can touch. Your body is like a house that gives shape to this space of peace and silence. When a house falls down, when its roof and walls collapse, no harm is done to the space inside. Only the boundaries have disappeared. In death we lose our bodily definition, but the space of inner peace, which some call the soul, is never harmed.

This is what dying unto death is all about. Devote some time in your day to going inward and finding your peace. It is waiting to be discovered. Once you find it, then you will not have panic in your eyes when death comes, because you will be entering a place that has grown familiar and even cherished.

Here are some suggestions for ways to grasp that death is not a dreaded enemy but an essential part of life:

ॐ Allow yourself to be near someone who is dying. Resist the fear that makes you shun them or stay away because you don't want to interfere.

ॐ Try to imagine your own death and then try to imagine your own birth. No matter how hard you try, both are impossible in any corner of your consciousness. There is no hint of a beginning or an ending. Consider, then, that your parents were not telling you the whole truth when they said you were born on a certain day. Inside we all feel ourselves as always having lived, which is true.

ॐ Go out into nature and stand by an old tree. Look up at it and realize that nothing you are seeing is stable or permanent. That solid trunk is a cloud of subatomic particles whirling in space, each one more than 99.9999% empty. As the tree shoots forth moisture and oxygen from its leaves, it forms a towering fountain of energy, something far more dynamic and alive than the wood and foliage you see with your eyes. Consider that this air and moisture are all it took to make a tree out of atoms born at the instant of the Big Bang. In no way does the tree own them, nor do they own it. All is flux, the ebbing and flowing in time or invisible energy packets. At what point, then, can you say that the tree is any more alive or any more dead than right now?

❧ Consider the possibility that death might be your greatest ally. When life wants to make a creative leap, it calls upon death to make it happen. Oxygen and hydrogen, for example, exist as invisible gases, yet when they bind into water, those properties cease to exist. Water is wet and fluid, and in bringing those qualities to life, nature sacrificed every semblance of gaseousness in oxygen and hydrogen. There was extinction of old forms to bring about the emergence of new ones never seen before. All creativity works this way. New and secret qualities never guessed at (who could guess at water's wetness even after millions of years looking at gases?) are waiting to be born. It is the joy of life to be part of their birth. This we know from every inventor, artist, mother, and saint.

❧

So, DO YOU choose to give yourself such joy? If so, then death is your greatest friend, because when you shed this body and personality, you are giving back to the source old outworn materials to be reshaped. You are not giving rise to a repeat of you, but to a new being that shoots forth with newly emergent qualities, qualities you in your current state cannot imagine. I believe fully in this view of death, which to me overrides any promise of heaven. Seeing the intimate love affair that life and death are conducting all around me, I cannot believe that it ends or that I have been excluded.

The Face of Evil

❧

THE MOST CONSTRICTED awareness belongs to those who do evil. Evil arises when there is a state of imbalance so severe that a person no longer values anyone else. Thus evil is an extreme form of egotism. *There is only my truth and my way*—such is the dogma of the fanatic, or the terrorist. But the abusive husband, the drug dealer preying on children, the mugger and murderer all feel equally cut off and numb.

It is possible to explain away evil. Emerson called it the absence of good, depriving evil of any rightful existence on its own. It is possible to transcend evil, as happened in the World Trade Center attacks when trapped workers phoned their loved ones, not to express their own horror but to offer reassurances. The most common message sent out in the face of death was "I wanted you to know that I am all right, and that I love you."

Yet when the buildings collapsed and violence was visited on thousands and thousands of innocent victims, evil won. I think back to the firefighters rushing up the stairs in the twin towers. "We were evacuating in an orderly way," said one survivor, recalling the brief time between the airplanes crashing and the ultimate collapse of the towers. "People lined up on the stairs, the lights were still on, and nobody seemed panicky even though the line moved slowly and often stopped. At one point I heard the freight elevator go by in free fall; people were screaming inside. As the firemen came up toward us, the line moved to one side and we all applauded, cheering them on. We still felt that we would be rescued. Yet in a few moments, those firemen would all be dead. I still see them, all the young, beautiful faces going by us as we clapped—all wiped out in a single stroke."

Physical violence seems like the evil that is most unforgivable. Reducing a person to body parts sickens us. When survival is threatened physically, the visceral response must have its way. In some cases outrage ends the discussion. Retaliation becomes the only order of business. Forgiveness must wait in line.

When you align with spirit, what you experience goes beyond the individual to something larger that we all share, an over-soul. No one is excluded from this over-soul, no matter how heinous their crimes. I found it extremely touching that the women of Bosnia, a place where savage hatred has endured for centuries, could still find a human connection that had no violence in it. When interviewed, they said they prayed for an end to violence, without resorting to the clichés of nation and ethnicity. Suffering purified them; they felt the suffering of other women who were supposed to be their enemies.

Yet when brave and innocent firemen are exterminated in the very act of offering help, evil isn't purifying. It is darkness come to earth, monstrous acts chosen freely and then carried out. Many personify this darkness as Satan. Some believe the Devil has a body and a face, others that he is more abstract. Terrorists and evildoers in general are said to be in the grip of this darkness. Men are known by what they do, and the slaughter of innocent lives does absolute harm.

The ancient scriptures of India declare that evil and wrong cannot survive in the vicinity of a saint. Without knowing if this is literally true, I take heart from it. Goodness is a positive force. None of the totalitarian horrors visited on humanity in the twentieth century lived to see their own triumph. Evil does perish, coming back into balance with the force of creation and evolution. The Berlin wall came down by the sheer weight, inertia, and exhaustion of repression.

Many people claim that this evolutionary process is too slow, that it amounts to passivity. I agree that sometimes active opposition to evil is necessary, but this doesn't mean one has to support the forces of destruction.

It is important to remember that anything you can do to expand your awareness will automatically counter evil. This includes all the healing work we have discussed. Be gentle when you are tempted to be harsh. Pay attention when you are tempted to turn a blind eye. Accept that the negativity you are feeling belongs to you when you are tempted to blame someone else.

Personal transformation on this level is the highest way to combat evil. The more conscious you become, the more you come into balance. Once balanced, you can choose to reject destruction; your awareness expands beyond the immediate hurt to see that evolution is eternal and therefore eternally possible.

We would all agree that anger gives rise to many evil acts, not anger per se, but anger that has become trapped. If your awareness is open and free, anger flows through it. This applies both to rage generated inside yourself when you feel victimized, and anger that comes from outside, in the form of attack. Both are meant to leave when their job is done. Anger's work is to alert your defense systems. Aggression and defense are part of the survival repertoire of almost every species that must compete to mate, find food, and occupy territory. What is unnatural is to hold on to rage. Festering, it feeds on itself and eventually breaks out in violence.

Every living system that goes out of balance attempts to right itself. This is true of your blood pressure and your heart rate but also of the rain forest or a population of birds. Pressure on the system from one side—such as lack of food, absence of home ground, or the sudden intrusion of enemies—causes a reaction to shove the system back into balance. Violence is the most extreme response to imbalance. Despite all the talk about human beings being innately violent, aren't we also innately gentle? The evidence for both is equally strong. So evil may come down to stress: being pushed so far beyond one's ability to cope that aggression has no choice but to push back. The appalling fact that the terrorists of September 11 were willing to commit suicide struck many as testimony to their absolute evil. I took it as a sign of absolute desperation. As individuals, none of these attackers could cope with a world that had injured them, to the point that survival wasn't an option anymore.

What of religious fanaticism? Isn't it evil? Yes, of course, but religion doesn't teach evil. It gets called into the service of evil once the mind is made up. The most recent brain studies from M.I.T. indicate that when people are asked to make moral decisions, it is the emotional center of the brain that increases in activity, instead of the rational centers layered higher up in the cortex. Only after anger emotionally fires us up do we call in the cortex to fashion reasons, including religious reasons.

In a savage irony, terrorists always feel righteous in their actions. The same is true for all the great evildoers in the twentieth century, from Hitler to Pol Pot. The wrongdoer holds him- or herself up as the victim. One sees this chillingly in everyday life. Abusive husbands who beat their wives always plead that they were driven to it. One sees interviews with violent muggers who blame the people they shot for not giving up their money when asked.

But if you plot revenge against an evildoer, you are harming yourself: Not because the thought may come back to injure you, which is superstition, but because negative thinking reinforces the source of negativity. Darkness adds to darkness. The simple psychological fact is that the mind grows from habit and use, and as long as you habitually use those centers that send out blame, anger, retribution, intolerance, and violence, those centers will be nourished in their growth.

Nurture instead the light that you find inside. Transformation doesn't come about by being touched with a magic wand. Habit and use apply here too. If you find even the smallest reasons for sending out intentions of love, tolerance, forgiveness, and peace, these centers will grow inside your mind. Spirit counts on this growth.

One question gets asked over and over. Why does God permit evil to exist? The answer, I feel, must be divine patience. God is waiting for us to grow into our goodness. God wants us to see on our own, so that the vision will endure. It may take a long time, but that is the price for having free will. No choice is forced upon us. There is only the allure of peace and love as higher realities.

Do we have proof that God is exerting an influence toward good? No one can convince another person that good will triumph over evil. The reality is that humans grow through experience. When the sinner grows tired of doing wrong, he tries on the experience of doing good, and in time a saint is born.

The poet Rumi, to whom I return season after season, wrote, "I live on the lip of insanity, knocking at the door, searching for reasons. / The door opens. / I have been knocking from the inside." It may sound strange, but evil becomes much less threatening when you stop seeing it outside in "them" and go inside yourself. There really isn't a "them," there is only "us," the spirits who delight in our freedom to do and feel anything, from the most sublime acts to the most atrocious. Jesus and Buddha didn't walk around teaching, "Become as good as I am." They looked into the common condition of humanity and became it. Total empathy led to total compassion. The empathy grew from tearing down the walls that the ego has built. The compassion grew from the inrushing of feelings that couldn't be denied. "Ah, so I really am you" is the revelation that every saint has in common.

Total compassion leads to total forgiveness. You can't force yourself to forgive anyone. Forgiveness doesn't belong to the mind. It is a feeling of the heart. So once again we face a paradox, for it appears that softening your heart and gently tending its wounds will protect you from evil. Building a fortress and defending yourself behind it will only make you more vulnerable. Healing your own heart is the single most powerful thing you can do to change the world. Your own transformation will enable you to withdraw so completely from evil that you contribute to it by not one word, one thought, or one breath. This healing process is like recovering your soul.

Recovering the Soul

✑

A MOTHER TRAVELING with her daughter stands impatiently at the ticket counter. Her vacation flight has been delayed. Can't something be done? Fingers click away at the computer—it turns out she can get on another flight. She smiles with relief, takes the new tickets, and rushes for the gate. A wife who is booked on a Wednesday flight decides to leave a day early, and she too is fortunate that seats are available. She looks forward to being together with her husband in a few hours. The slow tedium of airports prompts a father to while away some time by phoning home and chatting with his five-year-old son before he goes off to kindergarten. He hangs up with the words, "Daddy loves you," when they announce his flight.

In less than two hours, these people disappear from the

face of the earth. Where did they go? Did some part of them survive the tragedy? Death always creates anxiety about the soul. In those terrorist catastrophes people died without leaving remains that were recoverable. This made the tragedy even more agonizing for the survivors. A mother with five children at home was married to a firefighter who perished in the rescue efforts. When asked what she told her children, she said, "I told them we were lucky. At least we had the gift that his body was recovered."

The complete disappearance of someone you love is unspeakably terrifying. A primitive part of us believes in solid, material things as the touchstone of reality. The soul, if real, is entirely invisible. It is hard to believe in it with the same conviction that we believe in our physicality, the solid presence that is so reassuring while we are alive.

I found myself in this no man's land between doubt and belief when my father, who was in his eighties, suddenly died. Daddy-ji was gifted with a saintly personality; he was quiet and often self-effacing, someone who would rather listen than push himself forward. As he grew older, he worried deeply about my mother, who was growing more infirm in her old age than he was. One night in November he got out of bed and woke her up. In retrospect it became clear he was bidding farewell. He kissed my mother, softly returned to his room, and closed his eyes. Death came to him peacefully and with full awareness. As a way of leaving us, my father chose one of dignity and peace, making hardly a ripple.

Yet he left a huge hole in my heart. I wasn't prepared for this event, even though I thought I was. The family gathered in Delhi, and I experienced the rituals of death for the first time. I went to the *ghats*, the burning grounds by the river, and read rosters of all our ancestors, going back hundreds of years, who had been cremated there. It was left to me to oversee the burning of my father's remains, and I felt a kind of timeless comfort and personal dread. A burning ground smells of death. There is no escaping the shadow's presence, and although it is hard to set these words down before Western readers, when my father's ashes were still warm, I was called upon to disintegrate the crumbling shell of his skull with a stick. It was the final rite of release. In the distance I became aware of the sounds of a wedding band and boys playing cricket a hundred yards away. The continuity of life came home even at that grim moment.

When I witnessed the television spectacle of six thousand people disappearing instantly, I knew what the fireman's widow meant when she said that it was a gift to recover his body. It took months of reflection before I could answer for myself the question of where my father went. He was the loving person who had never been absent from my life, yet suddenly in his place was a void.

CAN AN INVISIBLE wisp of spirit be as real as our physical bodies? Things aren't real because you can see and touch them. That is an illusion of the senses. A granite cliff is real because invisible forces hold together invisible packets of energy. No one has ever seen gravity or the curvature of space, yet their existence is far more secure than granite, which will dissolve and cease to exist billions of years before gravity does. All the most real things, in fact, are invisible. No one has ever touched time. Truth leaves no fingerprints. Love escapes the five senses.

Recovering the soul, then, isn't a matter of trying to believe in some invisible ghost for the first time. Can we then trust in the invisible existence of the soul even though it cannot prevent the onset of pain, violence, and suffering?

The soul is best understood not as a wispy ghost but as your true self, present in you at this moment. You don't see it, although when you feel the impulse of love, you have contacted it. There can be no doubt that you have a self, therefore to step onto a new level, that of your true self, is not actually so formidable a task.

Each of us has developed a strong belief in a false self built up from the ego. Ego has already come up several times, but let me briefly summarize its value system through a few key words: limited, constricted, clinging, acquisitive, closed-off, and afraid. Just listing them makes it hard to believe that anyone would owe their allegiance to these values, but consider how much behavior is motivated by them.

The true self is of immediate value because it can fulfill needs that the ego cannot. These needs, mentioned earlier, are as follows:

The need for safety.
The need to belong.
The need to be acknowledged by others.
The need to matter.
The need to express yourself freely.
The need for love.

Desire and fulfillment are the natural rhythm of life. Each of these needs exists to be met. Your true self is already fulfilled, therefore when you merge with your true self, you will be able to feel completely wanted, safe, worthy, and loved. Expressing yourself will come naturally and freely. You will matter more than you ever imagined.

The ego sees the same needs and feels the same desire, but it reaches outside for fulfillment. People try to convince themselves that they matter if they have status and money. They feel they are expressing themselves if they can make their opinions heard. They try to belong by climbing the ladder of success. The strategy of reaching outward is the only one the ego knows. The true self knows only the strategy of going inward.

I have a friend who recently moved to the inner city of Boston, and when he walks to work, for the first time in his life panhandlers plague him. One after another they appear in his path, holding out their cups, calling out for spare change. "For a while," he said, "I ignored them, but it was impossible. One panhandler used to hold the door open when I went to the bank, and with thinly veiled sarcasm he'd say, 'Let me help you there. Maybe you'll remember me when you come out.' I resented this false politeness, and within weeks I hated all of them. Why couldn't I walk to work in peace without being accosted for handouts?"

After wrestling with his anger and guilt—for he did want to do the right thing—my friend had a brilliant idea. Why not simply give some money to anyone who asked him? "It worked amazingly well. I collected change in my pockets, and no matter who asked me, I gave something. Immediately my anger vanished. And then my eyes opened. I saw that these people really are lost and alone, and it is an act of cruelty for me to withhold the meager amount they want."

It feels remarkable when petty anger can be transformed to so noble a feeling as compassion. Yet in this case it happened in a moment, thanks to a simple shift in perception. The true self doesn't goad us into being good. It takes our existing impulses and views them in a new light. Insight opens

he gates of the heart. Many times a day each of us feels
he impulse, however faint, of saintliness. Walk down a city
street for ten minutes and you see all around you reasons
o give, to help, to offer charity and compassion, to forgive,
and perhaps even to love. In each situation, the need to cut
oneself off is present, because that has been a long habit, but
a fresher impulse also arises. The true self is sending these
new signals.

Notice and feel them. Dwell on them instead of pushing
hem down. Avoid your habit of turning away or being too
afraid to act. Act when you can. Appreciate your own goodness and congratulate yourself whenever you move closer, if
by an inch, to your true self.

That's the program, and it is a simple one. There is no need
to regard the soul as an abstraction handed down by theology.
It is an aspect of yourself waiting for your recognition.

The credo of the true self is joy with detachment. The joy
comes from no longer having to cling to a small, defended territory. The detachment comes from having such wide awareness that everything is at once yours and not yours.

In the wake of my father's passing, I kept asking myself if
he was simply extinguished, if the person I loved no longer
existed, had nowhere to go but into vast emptiness. I realized
that these doubts came from the emotional level, but what
of that? Emotions need to be satisfied as much as, if not more
than, the mind.

Then one day I stopped resisting the image of my father disappearing, and with a rush of relief I saw that he couldn't disappear because he had never been here to begin with. The soul, or true self, is not inside you, nor is it outside. Like gravity or truth or time, your soul is everywhere. Therefore at the moment of death it has nowhere to go—it has already arrived. Imagine a series of concentric circles, one within the other. Then imagine yourself living in each of these circles, beginning with the smallest.

The first circle is your body and the physical world of the five senses. Here you live in time as it passes.

The second circle is the pattern of brain waves that create your thoughts, feelings, and desires. Here you live in the mind.

The third circle is the invisible pattern of energy from which the brain was created. Here you live in the play of natural forces.

The fourth circle is the field that extends infinitely through the cosmos, from which all energy is born. Here you live in the fluctuating waves of the cosmic ocean.

The fifth circle is the silent, unmoving field that unites all force fields, from which space and time arose. Here you live within the ocean itself.

The sixth circle is the womb of the universe—infinite

dimensions wrapped within each other. Here you live in the cradle of creation before creation occurs.

❧ *The seventh circle* is the uncreated—God, Brahman, the One and All. Here you live eternally.

What I realized with a wave of relief was that no one has to go anywhere. *All these realms exist at the same time.* You and I meet on the street as two bodies, but we also meet as two minds, two souls, two citizens of the cosmos. Ultimately we do not meet at all—we merge into the ocean of spirit. We are one.

The only thing that changes is perception. You and I choose the circle we belong in, and once we identify it, we call that reality. Ego offers the most constricted reality, the innermost circle. Looking over the wall to a larger reality, or even to another person's point of view, ego says, "What has this got to do with me?" But ego does not exist to deny the soul. Ego exists because it is necessary.

The force of evolution tugs at us, coaxing us to see into larger circles. The source of this tugging is the soul, which already knows every layer of reality, from the deepest darkness to the eternal light.

For many centuries no one had the faintest idea about brain functioning or gravity or subatomic particles. The fact that we didn't perceive them doesn't mean they didn't exist. Rather, that infinitely expanded reality lay waiting for us to cross our own boundaries. As we did, perceptions shifted, giving birth to new worlds.

When you can experience grief and yet are able to come to recognize the work of the soul, you will feel elated. The hidden message of suffering will have revealed itself. For myself, I was able to accept the loss of my father in a completely new way—as no loss at all. He became more present to me than ever before. I felt that I was meeting his true self as I met mine. This was our soul connection. I had crossed a boundary that was very difficult on the level of feeling. My father's beloved face, his voice, his physical closeness were gone. I had deeply feared that he as an individual was also lost. Now I can celebrate that nobody has an individual self, not at the soul level. You and I roam the universe pretending to be individuals. Loss is a phantom projected by the ego, which believes only in the individual "I."

What are you and I, really? We are an expression of the entire universe. The universe gave birth to you and me as separate persons, but it didn't let us out of eternity's embrace. At this very moment we stand outside time as surely as inside it.

As much as you need the world in order to live, the world needs you in order to exist. You are the only way the universe can experience exactly the things you feel, see, touch, think, and desire as no one else can. Patterns arise and fall, passing away like dust. With one side of your being, you play in these patterns, creating dramas of light and dark. But with another side of your being you are pure awareness, pure creativity, pure possibility. You are the source. Therefore when you die, the same process occurs that led to your being born. The source rearranges the patterns once again. Look upon the afterlife as you look upon this instant, as both a new birth and a new death.

Recovering the soul is a journey from one circle of awareness to the next. Expansion of consciousness doesn't take you anywhere. You may have a life-changing insight on a Friday or in a specific place like Chicago or Jerusalem. But these are only bits of the passing scenery. The highest realms in which you live are nowhere and everywhere. The edges of time and space are hard when viewed from the inner circle, where the body strives to exist. The edges get softer in the domain of art and music, softer still in the domain of love.

Jesus described the journey with such beautiful conciseness when he said that freedom means "being in the world but not of it." Equally beautiful is the teaching of the Upanishads, which say that for someone in ignorance, experience is like writing in stone; for someone who has begun to know spirit, experience is like writing in water; for someone who is liberated, experience is like writing in air.

Joy with detachment is the spiritual aim of life. On the healing path you will experience moments of both, and there will be stretches when neither is possible. Your ego will shout its demands, and then "I, me, and mine" will have to be tended to. This is natural. The smallest circle of your being, the place of ego and its needs, is just as holy a place as the wider circles. To say that anyone has a false self is a relative term. It is more true to say that we are all writing our lives in stone, hoping for the day when we will be written in water, and knowing the time will come when we will be written in air.

PART II

A Hundred Days of Healing

My soul can lead me to healing.
I will become one with my true self.

WITH THIS FIRST AFFIRMATION we begin the healing process. From there ninety-nine other expressions of spirit follow, one for each day. All together they summarize the process of emotional and spiritual healing. They shift our attention from the external world to the inner world, which is the source of light. Suffering threatens to make life meaningless. That is its greatest danger, not the pain it inflicts. It is up to each of us to restore meaning. Doctors cannot do it for us with their medicine; friends cannot do it for us with their solace and comfort. You are healed when you can say to yourself, "I matter, I belong, I am worthy, I am safe, I can express myself, I am loved."

Inner healing involves moving from darkness to the light. "Light" is a word that has different meanings yet is generally understood as love and understanding. Love nurtures the emotional body; understanding fills the voids created by pain.

As you contact your true self, you will discover that the soul is not passive. Spirit knows more about us than we do ourselves, and it wants to support our every step toward wholeness. The soul journey has been called the pathless path because there is no map. Every person's steps are different.

But the great wisdom traditions have told us a multitude of helpful things about spirit. In the pages ahead I have extracted a hundred days of guiding thoughts—some in the form of affirmations, some as insights, lessons, and exercises—that have sparked self-healing for centuries. Each is a sutra, from the Sanskrit word for "thread," or, less literally, an aphorism that contains power.

Light has the power to fill the void afflicted by darkness. Healing yourself comes in two stages—releasing the energy of suffering, then replacing it with the soul's energy. It is a gentle process, very much like holding on to a thread as it leads you from step to step. What begins as the merest hint of new strength will grow. Your true self is always available to meet any challenge, find any answer, and show you the way out of any dilemma.

What matters is your connection to this true self. In fear and isolation your soul seems aloof, with no power at all. But this is a perception born of following the ego, which all of us have done. If you take the time to listen to the voice of the soul—where the ego is silent—you will be astonished at the power you have at your command, however long it has been overlooked. No other discovery in life is as joyful as regaining your true self. Falling in love is the only comparable event, yet it is temporary and depends on another person, the beloved. Your true self is forever and depends upon no one but yourself. When they say that suffering ennobles a person, this means that with the impetus of crisis, old habits and perceptions are uprooted. The unknown makes itself felt, and if you open yourself to it, the meaning of the soul reveals itself as a truth that you never anticipated before the crisis began. In this way every suffering is seen to contain a hidden spiritual message.

Day 1

My soul can lead me to healing.
I will become one with my true self.

This is an affirmation about the goal of the healing journey, which is unity. Use this affirmation—and the others that follow—by first reading it over. Absorb the words quietly. Close your eyes and repeat them to yourself. Take another moment as you breathe easily. Then read the words aloud. You can repeat them just a few times, or as often as feels natural. If you feel doubt or resistance, let it rise and fade away. Layers of resistance are normal. Get in touch with the part of yourself that understands and accepts the affirmation. End by offering gratitude to your soul, and ask that it bring you insight throughout the day.

At this moment my soul is with me.

It is as close as my breath.

This affirmation is about the nearness of the true self. Use this as your affirmation today, and each time you repeat it finish by breathing gently and seeing your breath as cool, calming, white light. *Breath is the movement of spirit in its subtlest physical expression. When you breathe gently and slowly, the body relaxes, the mind finds its still center, and the stage is set for inspiration—the flowing in of spirit.*

My soul is outside and inside.

The light is everywhere.

This affirmation is about seeing beyond physical boundaries. As you say this affirmation aloud, end by breathing gently and seeing soft white light emanating in all directions, filling every space in your body and every corner of your room.

My soul is my self.
It knows me and hears me.

This affirmation is about the soul's ability to listen. As you say this affirmation, end by imagining that your being extends in all directions, just as the light does. See your being filling your room, then your house, then the space around your house in all directions. All this is your domain. Since it is filled with spirit, it knows you and cares for you.

DAY 5

My true need is to know myself
as my soul knows me.

This affirmation is about the purpose of healing. When a person is in pain, there is great need, even more than in everyday life. We feel like lost children. A sense of abandonment and helplessness is normal. But these needs are a memory of the past. They repeat what you felt as a child. Your true need right now is for knowledge and power. To heal, you must understand, and once you understand, you need the energy to recover from pain and move on.

*My soul knows me as
complete and whole.*

This affirmation is about gaining a new self-image that is not divided. Wholeness is defined simply as the one thing that remains the same even when everything else is changing. That one thing is spirit. Its presence is felt as joy with detachment. Your true self sees you that way.

My soul knows me as gentle.

This affirmation is about the need not to use force. Say this affirmation, then try to know yourself as gentle. Observe yourself saying a kind word or performing a gentle, comforting act. This could be as simple as a thank you, a touch on the shoulder, a word of understanding. See how this feels to you. Be with it. Ask that such moments come more often. You are acting from your true self.

DAY 8

My soul knows me as peaceful.

This affirmation is about the need not to be angry. After saying this affirmation, know yourself as peaceful. At some point during the day, when you catch yourself feeling angry, remind yourself that this isn't you. Let the angry energy pass through like a visitor who isn't being allowed to stay. Let it have its say, but know that your allegiance lies elsewhere, with your true self.

My soul knows me as lacking nothing.

This affirmation is about being sufficient within your self to meet any challenge. Use this as your affirmation today. Then as you go about your routine, notice all the things you want to buy or cling to or possess as your own. Don't judge these impulses; just be aware of them. Remind yourself that things will come and go in your life, but you were born in fullness that lies within you. It lacks nothing. Is there an underlying anxiety beneath the desire? The ego wants to acquire things out of insecurity, out of a sense of lack. Remind yourself that everything comes and goes except the soul. It's from the soul that a person gains a sense of inner fulfillment. The soul lacks nothing and therefore has no anxiety about the outside world: gain is not a need, loss is not a threat.

My soul knows me as joyful
because I am free.

This affirmation is about freedom. After saying this affirmation, practice not clinging to anything for the rest of the day. Not clinging means accepting whatever happens without protest or resistance. Through acceptance you make yourself available. You are saying, "I give you permission to be with me as I am with myself." Acceptance puts other people at ease, which in turn makes love possible. If you are full and complete in yourself, if you lack nothing, if your desires come and go easily, you will always be free. In this freedom there is total joy. You cannot be hurt, not in your true self.

I will see everyone else as I see myself.

This affirmation is about perception. After saying this affirmation, ponder it for a moment. People are different in many ways that can't be denied. We look different; we have different tastes and backgrounds. If you focus on differences, as the ego does, you can't escape the tendency to feel better or worse than someone else. This is the game of comparison, and comparison always leads to judgment. Yet without trying to erase any differences you don't have to play the game of comparison. Permit everyone to have what you have: wholeness. See with the eyes of your true self and know that if you are complete, everyone else must also be complete.

I will nurture every need but one—
the need to judge others.

This affirmation is about releasing the need to be judgmental. Make this your lesson for today. Consider what happens when you judge someone: it makes another person wrong. Someone else is wrong to feel a certain way, to look a certain way, to hold certain opinions. Judgment immediately creates separation. Any person who is wrong becomes "them." The need to judge arises from the need to be isolated—this is the ego's form of defense. But at the same time you are pulling away from your true self. The same walls that keep other people out also shut off the flow of spirit. When you learn not to judge, you are basically saying, "I am willing to let anything in without deciding first whether it is good or bad." In the practice of openness, you will be inviting your soul to be intimate with you.

I will not resist others.

This affirmation is about overcoming obstacles. Make this your practice for today: try to listen to people you usually ignore, accept a suggestion or a compliment you might brush off, look with open eyes at someone whose appearance strikes you unpleasantly. Feel this openness, which will always be countered by its opposite tendency, the tendency to remain isolated. Is your resistance to openness strong or weak? Does it feel good to resist? With practice, you will find that not resisting holds the secret to many spiritual experiences, including the ability to love.

DAY 14

I will not resist myself.

This affirmation is about self-acceptance. Make it your practice for today to stop rejecting any aspect of yourself that you dislike and push away. The most common forms of resistance are denial and repression. Denial says, "I don't really feel anything." Repression says, "I am not permitted to feel." So today, when you run across ordinary irritants or stresses, feel what comes up. When you see something beautiful or heartwarming, feel what comes up. Catch yourself if you are in the habit of dismissing your feelings. Let your response blossom as it wishes. Most especially, don't take your first reaction as final. Denial and repression step in to close the emotions' gates at the speed of thought. Mentally return two or three times to any situation that aroused a response, and watch the deeper layers unfold.

My true self responds with love.

This affirmation is about seeing a spiritual truth. Think about the nature of love today. Love has two faces: personal and impersonal. Personal love is felt as long as "I" get something—pleasure, validation, agreement, acknowledgment for being important—so it is rooted in the needs of the ego. Giving your personal love to someone else requires an agreement, an exchange, and a bargain with that person. If either side breaks the bargain, love is cut off. Impersonal love arises from the true self, which needs to exact nothing from anyone else. Impersonal love doesn't mean indifference to others but extending your embrace beyond personality and ego. Such love brings intense pleasure with no price to pay. You owe no one for your happiness. Being untied from ego gives the soul great freedom. Whatever it sees, it can find love in that thing. While the ego is reacting with fear, anger, clinging, greed, avoidance, hatred, violence, or aggression, the true self feels only the steady flow of impersonal love. Affirm this today, and know that the soul's love awaits you.

*I will see one thing today as if for the
first time.*

This affirmation is about newness. Make this today's promise to yourself. Pause to see one thing with the same appreciation that you felt the first time you laid eyes on it. Your soul sees every experience through new eyes. It isn't the things around you that have become tired or stale, but your perception that has made them fade away. Notice how swiftly you decide whether you like or dislike anything. Some old memory is telling you how to react. You know in advance what you like and dislike, what will be accepted or rejected. But you have the choice not to go there. In the tiny gap before you react—or in the pause afterward—you can be open. Ask your soul for its response, which is always to appreciate. Today give yourself permission to apply new feelings of appreciation to a flower, a curtain fluttering in the breeze, a child's game, a tree gracing the roadside—anything you have taken for granted which calls out to be seen anew.

DAY 17

I will nourish someone with light.

This affirmation is about communication. Make this your practice for today: feel an impulse of loving awareness, and then make it your gift. Send your impulse of love to a person in need, a person you already love, or all people in the world. Then let go. Your gift will be received in the spiritual bank where light is gathered.

DAY 18

I will lift my judgment against someone.

This affirmation is about forgiveness. Make this your practice today: think of one person you have judged against, and then take your judgment back. Find any words you want: *I'm sorry; I didn't mean that; I've changed my mind; I take back whatever has hurt you.* But these shouldn't merely be words. Be in a loving space so that you really intend to make amends with sincerity. Thoughts by themselves have the power to wound. By taking back a negative thought, you offer healing.

My every thought has the power either to wound or to heal.

This affirmation is about spiritual energy. Make this your lesson today: when you hold a thought about someone, you are either drawing them near or pushing them away. The power that draws people near is love. When you hold anyone in loving awareness, your natural instinct is to embrace, and whoever is embraced is being released from separation. Fear pushes people away. Anyone you push away is being told to go back into separation. Your thoughts may seem like small things, yet each person occupies a fragile space emotionally and is easily wounded. Today welcome everyone into the light that you can. This is vital to your healing and theirs.

*I will use my thoughts wisely and
respect their power.*

This affirmation is about taking responsibility. After saying this affirmation, end by sitting still and consciously bringing everyone you know into your awareness. See them coming together in a town square. Imagine that you are the ruler of this gathering, with the power to hurt or benefit anyone you wish. Now look over all the faces gazing up at you and say, "I will use my power wisely." In this promise you acknowledge your role in everyone's healing. You offer your thoughts to the service of spirit.

I ask the universe to listen.

I need to matter.

This affirmation is about reaching beyond boundaries. Make this your request for today. The need to be heard is different from needing attention. You are surrounded by infinite intelligence, which is available every moment. Begin to draw upon it by asking to be heard. If you consciously ask a higher intelligence to take notice of you, over time you will notice that it does. Things you want to have happen will come about more easily, as if shaped by an invisible hand. Your true self sees nothing magical in such mastery of time and space. Although it works invisibly, the magic is actually you. So tell the universe today that you need to matter, and it will take heed.

I can find my soul here and now.

This affirmation is about the present moment. Make this your promise for today: try to be as present as you can, and when you become aware that you have wandered from the present, ask to be brought back. The mind easily slips out of the now. We fantasize about the future. We reminisce about the past. When we feel distressed we anticipate the pain to come or remember the pain that went before. Each detour takes us out of the present. Yet the here and now is the only meeting place where you will find your soul.

This moment is the still point around which everything turns.

This affirmation is about focus. Make this your lesson for today: everything around you is constantly on the move. As you chase after events, you keep postponing the day when you can stop. But stopping only happens right now. The reason for stopping is to appreciate what the now contains, which is stillness. Inside stillness lies a treasure. It can be opened using nothing more than silent awareness—the gaze of the soul. If you wish to open your soul's treasure, regard the present moment as a uniquely precious thing—the still point around which the world revolves.

I ask myself for rest and peace.

This affirmation is about attention. Make this your practice today: give your attention only after bringing it to rest inside. All the things that are coming your way today call for your attention. You can pay attention in two ways—from a place of action, which is the restless mind, or from a place of stillness, which is the peaceful mind. You always have this choice. Your mind by nature may seem restless, but its deeper nature is to be calm. Today, as you become aware that your attention is scattered, restless, on the move, discontented, or focused on external things like schedules and deadlines, stop and choose. Ask for a peaceful place from which to view the very next thing. Stop the internal dialogue with its constant chatter and pressure. Know that the reason to have restful awareness is that this is your true self.

I honor my stillness.

This affirmation is about values. After saying this affirmation, go about your routine, keeping faith with what you honor. Cherish the fact that you can stop anytime you wish and be at peace, even if only for a few moments. By honoring stillness, you are touching one piece of the soul's treasure.

I will be open to the support that spirit is giving.

This affirmation is about guidance. Make this today's promise to yourself, to look inside for guidance. Everyone needs support, and generally we look outside ourselves—to family, friends, coworkers, and like-minded people—for validation. This kind of support makes you feel that you are right. The ego gets assurance that you are not alone. But spirit wants to develop uniquely. It sends support to the inner person. Instead of making you feel that you are right, spiritual support adds to your sense of being free, at peace, loving, and aware. Be open to those feelings, because openness is the first step to transformation.

I will value the support that spirit is giving.

This affirmation is about spiritual self-worth. Make this today's promise to yourself: when you feel moments of being uncertain and alone, tell yourself that you have the same worth as your soul. In situations where you feel the urge to assert, disagree, or resist, don't follow that impulse. Find your own peace; accept the situation, and then watch. Do you see signs that what you want out of the situation can happen without resistance or assertiveness? When you value the support spirit is giving, the grip of ego is loosened immediately. You are capable of seeing any situation as spirit sees it, not just as ego does. If you value that capacity, it will grow.

We are contained in each other.

Therefore I can understand anyone as myself.

This affirmation is about shared humanity. Human nature is handed out one person at a time, yet we all share it. Ego tries to ignore the second half of that statement. It rushes into any situation with the assumption that "I" have the most important ideas, feelings, and perceptions. Spirit sees all thoughts as shared, all feelings as shared, and all perceptions as shared. This is a tremendous gift. Your capacity to see the world from beyond your own boundaries is precious—the true self will help you to gain a wider perspective if you are open to it. Give yourself permission to expand. Be aware of how others view a situation. When perception is fully aware, love and compassion enter spontaneously.

We are contained in each other.
Therefore I can accept anyone as myself.

This affirmation is about including other people. Shared experience excludes no one. Even those we label as evil or as wrongdoers are enclosed in the whole drama. The ego plays out one drama at a time, saying, "This is what's happening to me, everything else comes second." But in truth the whole drama is happening to you. Your conscious mind tunes in to one small scene, yet at deeper levels you are participating in everything that goes on—not just *my* happiness, *my* sorrow, *my* triumph, *my* understanding, but the happiness, sorrow, triumph, and understanding of humanity. Your next thought adds to the shared experience we will all tap into; the next thoughts of countless people you've never met are adding to your next experience. This is what it means to be contained within each other. Once you see that experience is always shared, you can accept others, however different they appear to be, as yourself.

We are contained in each other.
Therefore I can love anyone as myself.

This affirmation is about communion. Love is the next step after acceptance. Try this today. See someone without having any opinion at all—perhaps a child playing in the park or a diner sitting in a café, at a table for one. Tune in to the simple being that each of us shares. Isn't there love in appreciating a passing face, a gesture, or a glance? When you consider someone without assumptions, your inner antenna picks up a new signal. Instead of tuning in to someone's personality, you tune in to his or her essence. This essence is spirit, and when you detect it, the natural response is love.

I am not my body; my body is recycled earth.
I am not my breath; my breath is recycled air.
I am not my emotions; my emotions are
recycled energy.
I am not my thoughts; my thoughts are
recycled information.

These linked affirmations are about identification. As you say each one, experience your body, your breathing, your emotions, and your thoughts. Each of these belongs to you, but they are not who you are. You are the one who observes them. You are the experiencer behind the experience. As matter and energy are recycled through you, everything is in flux except the true self, which organizes life like the choreographer of a dance, guiding every step without walking onstage herself.

I am not my ego; my ego is isolated and alone.
I am not my personality; my personality is a
combination of relationships.
I am the unchanging observer.

This affirmation is about the reality of "I." At the soul level you are a silent witness who experiences the world with joyful detachment. That is a real experience, one you can share. But to have it, the claims of ego and personality must be overcome. Their claim is that "I" is a being who is born and dies, who lives inside your body, and who is affected by the constant changes in its world. Fighting against this assertion will not work, because ego and personality want to survive beyond all else, and have many strategies for doing so. Allow them to be what they are. Your ego represents individuality in separation; your personality represents an amalgam of all the relationships you have had since you were born. Yet be aware that you stand apart from both. In moments of quiet awareness, know that you are the silent witness. You are the inward dweller that is the source of all experience.

DAY 33

In stillness I find my true self.

This affirmation is about awareness. As you go about your day, be mindful of your awareness. Sometimes it will be restless and active. This usually occurs when outside events press in, asking for reactions. But at other times your awareness will be still within itself. You will watch instead of act. You find yourself being the observer, and from the perspective of your soul, that is who you really are. Activity comes and goes, but the observer is steady and ever present. As you begin to identify with the observer, you will become less attached to things that change. The unchanging is truly who you are.

As the observer, I feel no need
to blame anyone.

This affirmation is about injustice. We blame others because we feel unjustly treated. Our anger and resentment comes from a real source of hurt—this isn't deniable. But what has been hurt is the ego. "I" feel injured, and to the ego that cannot be forgiven. The silent witness is not hurt, and therefore it feels no need to blame. When you take its perspective, you can sympathize with the ego's sense of injustice, as you would when a child is hurt, not expecting to change its point of view. Just as you comfort a child, comfort your ego, while at the same time preserving the viewpoint of spirit, which sees all pain and pleasure as parts of the passing scene.

As the observer, I hold all parts of myself
in loving awareness.

This affirmation is about reassurance. If you go through every aspect of yourself, you will find that each part has its own need for reassurance. Your ego tries to be reassured by being right as much as it can—"I" feels insecure when it feels either wrong or wronged. Your personality finds reassurance when it is accepted in relationships. It is made insecure by differences between people. Your mind finds reassurance in understanding—it feels insecure when it cannot comprehend an idea. Your body feels reassured when there is balance and absence of pain. Your emotions feel reassured when they find happiness and absence of conflict. Given all these differing needs, it would seem that there is no common ground, yet there is. When held in loving awareness, each aspect feels reassured. Ego, personality, body, mind, and emotions metabolize love on their own level. Knowing this, the observer provides loving awareness as the most powerful form of healing. You are doing this at every moment, and as you become intimate with your true self, you will do this more and more.

As I give loving awareness, so I receive it also.

This affirmation is about receiving. At the soul level love is a steady state, radiating the same energy all the time. You are in a constant state of giving. Since other people, at the level of their souls, radiate the same loving awareness, you are constantly receiving as well. For many it is harder to receive than to give. At the root of this discomfort is the ego, which feels strong when it is the provider but weak when it is in need. You don't have to accept its interpretation, however. Regard loving awareness as a free exchange between your soul and all others. Receive as freely as you give, without obligation. Loving awareness is a natural state that you are learning to appreciate in yourself more and more.

I do not have to join the clash of egos.

This affirmation is about conflict. At the ego level there must be conflict, because "I" knows itself by clashing against another "I." This clash brings about many forms of evil. War is a vastly expanded version of "I" against "I." Bigotry and prejudice depend upon the same conflict on a social level. Hatred in the name of God is actually disguised ego: your God is unacceptable because he doesn't agree with mine. You do not have to participate in this clash of "I" against "I." As your true self you feel contained in others; therefore you have no stake in protecting your own point of view. With that realization the source of conflict is healed.

I have no need to defend my point of view.

This affirmation is about tolerance. Merely tolerating another person is a distortion of true tolerance. True tolerance comes about when you no longer have to defend your own point of view. You can honor someone else's while yet not adopting it. To reach such a position means you have discarded judgment, which insists that one viewpoint must be right and another wrong. You must also discard attachment, which says that *my* opinion must be valued first and foremost. With these two steps, the basis for defending your point of view disappears. At the soul level you have already taken both steps, because your true self has experienced every point of view. It sees them as equal products of the isolated "I," and therefore subject to constant change. There is no reason to defend the shifting sands of ego and personality as if it was solid ground.

I am enriched by all points of view.

This affirmation is about inclusion. The ego feels safe whenever it has a chance to exclude. Dividing experience into "mine" and "not mine" is the ego's job. Let that be as it is, but know that your job is to enrich yourself with as much of life's bounty as possible. Your true self doesn't need experience to fill a void; it loves the panoply and drama of life the way an art collector loves the images he collects. An art collector feels enriched when he is able to absorb these images, but he doesn't mistake himself for his pictures. Likewise, you can be enriched by the points of view all around you without mistaking them for yourself. A viewpoint is just a perspective, a focus. Each varied focus is like a new image to a photographer—you snap the picture, appreciate it in the moment, and then wait for a new image to come along.

The highest point of view is appreciation.

This is the viewpoint of God.

This affirmation is about creativity. People have tried to approach God through many forms of worship, trying to imagine how God's mind works so that they can be holy in their own lives. We are told that God created the world and then took time to see that His work was good. He was appreciative. Appreciation may not often be used to describe a spiritual state, yet appreciation is in many ways the highest state. When you appreciate you don't put yourself first. You have nothing of ego at stake. Appreciation brings loving awareness to Creation. In seeing how beautiful something is, you are gazing at the divine. The deeper your appreciation, the more you are seeing with the eyes of the soul.

I will appreciate myself, including my pain.
Everything adds to the richness of the self.

This affirmation is about humility. Humility is the modesty that comes naturally when you see how vast creation is in all its infinite abundance. In India it is said that humility bows down before God like a tree laden with ripe fruit. The ego fears being made humble. The "I" is insecure and does not welcome being taken down to a lower position. The way to escape this attitude is by appreciating the richness of your self. Within you the drama of life plays itself out as in no one else. You can access the full range of experience, including experiences of pain and suffering. Even as you move to heal yourself, remain aware that the play of light and dark adds to the richness of life.

I ask my shadow self to emerge.
This is the first step of healing it.

This affirmation is about "the dark side." We are all aware of having dark impulses, which include hatred, fear, and aggression. These impulses arise from the unconscious, and our normal response is to keep them there. We push the dark side out of sight, yet it doesn't go away. It seeks expression, as all energies will. Healing isn't possible when dark energies are kept bottled inside. To begin healing, invite the shadow self back into your awareness. This isn't the same as acting out rage or terror or revenge. You are only sending a message that you are no longer shunning the shadow self; you are acknowledging its right to exist.

My shadow self is serving me.
I am grateful for that.

This affirmation is about repression. Your shadow self has gained the power to frighten you because you have repressed it. But the shadow doesn't see itself as an enemy. It sees itself as your guardian. It protects you by holding on to those energies that belong to you even though you feel guilty and ashamed of them. Guilt made you turn to repression as a solution. Shame makes you not want to look or listen when these energies call out. Because the shadow energies got pushed out of sight, they never had a chance to show you their hidden spiritual message. This message was for your growth, and thanks to the shadow self, who has held on to these old, forgotten experiences, you can revisit them. As the shadows of rage, fear, terror, and revenge return, you only need to see and understand. As soon as you do that, they will deliver their message and then go. This is the whole process of healing the shadow self.

I will ask the dark energies to teach me.

This affirmation is about facing fear. Like the shadow self, your fear doesn't see itself as harming you. It, too, believes that it is a safeguard. Stored in everyone's memory are past experiences of terror. By reminding you of those feelings, fear is trying to protect you from repeating the traumas of the past. As long as you push down your fear, you will not be able to receive it as an ally. But by the same token you can't just act on the basis of fear. At the soul level you see no need for fear, because you don't need protecting. Living in the now poses no threat, and referring to the past therefore serves no purpose. It is safe to go into your fear and ask it where it came from and what it wants you to know. Having seen the world from its perspective, reassure yourself that the soul needs no guardian. Learn from fear, heal it, and ask it to leave.

*My shadow self and I have the same goal—
to rejoin the light.*

This affirmation is about duality. Light and dark appear as opposites, and we've all learned to think of them as warring enemies. Duality is based on separation, yet the soul exists in harmony with everything, even darkness. Your shadow self knows this. As it holds negative energy for you, it tries to attract your attention, not to make you afraid or enraged or vindictive, but so that you can convert those feelings into understanding. Understanding is the light.

*Instead of rejecting my suffering, I will ask for it
to be transformed.*

This affirmation is about alternatives. Many emotions are difficult to feel, and those associated with suffering are the most
difficult—the heavy weight of sorrow, the stabbing pain of lost
love, the doomed apprehension of a grave illness. These are
long-term feelings and do not dissipate easily. One must live
with them until they are finished. Your soul can aid you in
healing by the process of transformation. Ask for spirit to work
on your pain by detaching you from it, by delivering its hidden
meaning, and by finding the way back to joy. In the middle of
suffering there is an overwhelming instinct to reject the pain
through denial, numbing and repression, yet these will only
make it stay longer. Stay with your feeling, not in order to
suffer, but to ask spirit for guidance; transformation is always
possible, even in the most intense situations. Be open and ask
without expectation. Allow solace to come from any direction.
Know that your true self does not wish you to be in pain for
any reason except as part of your spiritual journey.

All suffering can be released as energy.

This affirmation is about being objective. For all of us, suffering is intensely subjective. When pain is intense, it gives rise to thoughts of every kind, from despair and resignation to intense anger and struggle. This intense anguish wraps around the sufferer. Yet there is an objective way to handle suffering, which is not to dwell on thoughts and feelings but to consider all pain as energy. You can learn to disregard the voice of suffering, which offers no real healing. Go instead to your most centered, calm, objective place inside, and ask for release of the energies at the root of your pain. There is no condition immune to the soul's touch. This is not necessarily a rapid process, though it can be. Energy healers exist in every city, so the task doesn't have to be undertaken in isolation. The first step is to ask for objectivity—summon spirit to bring you out of emotional turmoil into a clear understanding of how these painful energies can be removed. Then be alert and wait for signs of guidance from inside or outside yourself—any avenue of help is possible.

DAY 48

I will release any hidden need to suffer.

This affirmation is about giving yourself permission to heal. There is no question that spirit wants to transform your pain and lift it completely. But it cannot act without your permission, because free will is always honored by your soul. You must be certain that you want suffering to end. It is hard to understand why anyone would cling to it, but at some level pain may be bringing you a secondary gain. Suffering makes the "I" feel noticed, important, the center of attention. It relieves the need to take care of oneself or to face difficulties or crises. All of these secondary reasons need to be resolved before the soul's healing can freely enter (although they are not enough to block it entirely). Declare your willingness today not to cling to any ulterior motive that prolongs pain.

Whatever benefit I may gain from suffering,
I can find without suffering.

This affirmation is about paths not taken. Whatever "good" effect you may be gaining through your suffering, a healthier path exists that requires no pain. The ego has many needs. When a person feels too guilty or ashamed to admit that a childish need still exists, suffering can come to the rescue. The person finds a painful way to get gratification without asking directly, a strategy that is usually unconscious. There is no need to judge yourself if your pain has a component of neediness. Judgment has always been the problem; it will never be the solution. Ask your soul to bring you what you really want. Perhaps you are crying out for love, waiting to be rescued, or asking to be acknowledged. These are legitimate feelings that spirit can answer.

*T*ransformation *is always possible.*

This affirmation is about shifting your inner landscape. Once any blockage is removed, everything inside you is ready to change. When you move a mountain the whole landscape shifts. Instead of leaving a hole, released energies leave new possibilities behind, but you have to seize them. Don't ask yourself for a total emotional makeover. When old energies of pain leave, there will always be an insight, and this becomes your clue for what to do next. For example, when "I need to suffer this way" is gone, the insight might be that you can take up music again or exchange a negative friend for a more positive one or explore a new city. These shifts in the outer landscape reflect a shift in the inner. Transformation is rarely like Cinderella turning into a princess in a flash—it occurs in a chain of new possibilities, one stitch at a time. When all the links are there, you will have achieved the total transformation. Countless insights are open to you. They will all be of the form "I can now do what I thought I couldn't before." At the end of the path, these small steps turn into, "I know the reality of God, who I thought was never there before."

DAY 51

I will ask to learn the ways of spirit.

This affirmation is about changing allegiances. As the result of long habit and conditioning, we know the ways of the ego all too well. If the ways of the soul are different, they too must be learned. The process is more conscious than when we were children, following the dictates of "I, me, mine." Then we had no other perspective, while as adults we must adapt to new thoughts, feelings, responses, and perceptions, replacing those that have grown familiar over the years. Today's affirmation expresses your dedication to learn these new ways—you are turning your allegiance from the outer to the inner world.

DAY 52

In spirit awareness comes first.

This affirmation is about consciousness. In spiritual terms, consciousness begins with the soul. It is pure awareness, all encompassing, silent, knowing, unborn, ever the same. Because we are all united at the source, every person can achieve this state of awareness. It is not inside or outside us but beyond both. To be fully aware places a person at the switchboard where body and mind are both created. You cannot gain the soul's awareness immediately, but it is always trying to contact you. By expanding your own awareness, you open the channels of communication. Today's affirmation acknowledges that awareness is the primary basis for dealing with all challenges. The soul can lead you into action—it is not simply passive—but action based on consciousness. This action is known in the great wisdom traditions as spontaneous right action, which means the right response to every situation as it occurs. It isn't impulsive or governed by habit. All the ways of spirit, whether they affect body, mind, or soul, originate in consciousness.

he soul's awareness is deeper than thought.
By contacting it, I will know what is best
in any situation.

This affirmation is about order and organization. Being the source of everything, spirit takes responsibility for organizing all situations and circumstances. This order runs much deeper than anything the intellect can devise. The cells in your body, for example, perform billions of precisely calibrated operations per second. Outer reality, which includes the events of your day, is organized from the same source. When you enter any situation, your actions can be in line with this deeper orderliness, or you can act from ego, imposing your own assumptions about what should happen. The soul also wants results, but it has wide vision; instead of thinking through a situation one step at a time, the soul arranges the entire package of cause-and-effect at the same time. By contrast, the thinking mind tries to manipulate results to suit what seems best for "I, me, mine." Ask for guidance that goes beyond thinking. Healing is possible from every direction and in many circumstances. Today you are affirming your faith in a wider vision.

I will learn how to contact my source.
The first step is quiet awareness.

This affirmation is about meditation. Meditation is the practice of going inward to access awareness that is deeper than thought. Meditation isn't just a time for peace and quiet, although both are needed. You are returning to your source. Make it your habit to find time alone, preferably once in the morning and once in the evening, in which you can close your eyes and go inside. There are many forms of meditation. A simple but effective one is meditation on the heart. Sit quietly for a moment, placing your attention on your heart, at the center of your chest under the breastbone. When you are settled, repeat the word "peace" silently, and see its influence radiating out from your body in all directions. Do this three times, and then say the word "happiness" the same way. Repeat three times, then go on to "harmony," "laughter," and "love." For longer medi-tations, you can use these words for as long as you like. Start with five minutes a session and work up to half an hour. Sit quietly for a few minutes after each session with eyes closed and simply appreciate the simplicity of quiet awareness.

I will wait for awareness to guide me.

This affirmation is about attunement. Meditation brings your mind into closer contact with its source, but decisions and choices need to be made outside meditation. In order to remain in touch with your source, you must stay attuned. If you are aware, your soul can contact you anytime, not just while you are sitting with your eyes closed. When someone says, "I ask my heart what is the right thing to do" or "I act on instinct"or "I know intuitively what is right for me," they are voicing their attunement. You need to find your own kind of focus. The process is personal. It's helpful, however, to know which signals to pay less heed to. Any impulse to defend yourself is not coming from your true self. Negative emotions that cloud the mind are not coming from the soul, nor is any response that is calculating what "I, me, mine" are going to gain. The soul's awareness is clear and pure; its rightness is detached, almost impersonal. Your soul isn't asking you to be cheerful, upbeat, and optimistic all the time. It is asking you to be as real as possible from the spiritual level, the basis of all reality.

*In every situation I will do the best I can
to follow the soul's insight.*

This affirmation is about the difference between thought and awareness. Right now you are aware of many things that require no thought. You are aware of being tense or relaxed. If pressure is being put on you, you are aware that this is different from being unconstrained. Thinking doesn't come into that kind of knowledge. Begin your attunement to the soul by checking what you are really aware of. If you feel free to make choices unaffected by outside influence, and if you are relaxed in mind and body yet alert at the same time, you are very close to spirit. Of course, it isn't possible to be in a pure state of spiritual awareness every time you have to make a choice or meet a challenge. You can notice, however, how spirit guides you when it does, and when you do feel tense or pressured, know that you are doing the best you can to reach your true self. Your awareness will expand if you put your faith in it.

I will prepare the way for insight by releasing any energy that blocks it.

This affirmation is about strategy. When it is fully developed, your awareness will respond as easily and quickly as you now respond from ego. For the present, while working with less expanded awareness, it helps to have a strategy. The purpose of the strategy is to get past knee-jerk responses and the ego's need to control. Insight always wants to come in; you only need to prepare the way. The way is blocked by anger, resentment, guilt, or fear. If you are feeling any of these emotions, then close your eyes and be fully aware of your feelings as sensations in your body. Tell yourself it's okay to have these feelings, but also ask yourself if you are willing to let them go. If and when you do let them go you will experience the light of your soul where insight and inspiration reside. True insight leads to inspiration, which is to be in touch with spirit, and then you are unstoppable.

I will be open to answers from any direction.
I know that spirit works through every channel.

This affirmation is about personification. In our lives we all
have people we trust and people we don't. We look on one person as a friend and ally, another as neutral or even as an enemy.
But spirit doesn't make such divisions. A stranger on the street
or next to you on the bus may offer you a wealth of answers and
insights. Healing comes from all directions because your soul
pervades everything. Seek a wise or authoritative voice if one is
available, yet be open to all possibilities. This includes following your inner voice, which may guide you in directions that
friends and family would never consider.

When I feel opposition, I will not oppose in return.

This affirmation is about nonresistance. The biblical injunction to turn the other cheek makes little sense to your ego. When it feels pushed, "I" wants to push back. When it is harmed, it wants to lash out against the attacker. In this way the cycle of attack and defense never ends. The soul's approach is not to oppose, which means not defending your position when a situation defies your expectations. Let the opposition pass, either by waiting or leaving or surrendering to the obstacle. The essence of this strategy is to put an end to struggle and conflict by allowing spirit to find its own way to the solution. You aren't required to be passive, however. You will only discover this when you refuse to oppose. In many cases a solution will appear as if magically, which is a sign that you are learning to act from the level of your true self.

DAY 60

When I feel the urge to struggle,
I will stop and wait for guidance.

This affirmation is about efficiency in action. In our society we have glorified struggle, as if getting anything the easy way is cheating. In truth spirit arranges the easy way, out of love for us. It is important to realize that you deserve to fulfill your needs easily. Don't glorify the pain and struggle that arise from the ego's limited vision. Expect the best outcome for yourself in any situation, and then accept with grace the result that you receive. It is the best you can do at this stage of your path.

*In all circumstances I want to act
with the least effort.*

This affirmation is about acting from pure awareness. Pure awareness is the same as the awareness you now have, but its scope is infinite. Pure awareness isn't bound by time; it knows no obstacles. When you have a desire, all solutions are known at the level of your soul. These vary in how easy they are to attain. If you want a new car, having one miraculously appear in your driveway is one possibility, but more likely is an outcome in which you work for the money to buy the car. However, by precluding the possibility of miracles the ego has tied itself to struggle, thereby overlooking the infinite power of spirit. To change this situation, shift your expectations. Ask to achieve your desires with the least effort. Spirit will uphold this shift more and more as you learn how to live from the basis of nonstruggle. In time you will be doing much less to receive much more. At the level of the soul, you already possess everything by doing nothing at all.

I will achieve everything first in consciousness.

This affirmation is about gestation and birth. Desires ripen in the womb of the unconscious before they manifest in physical reality. In this process each desire moves through layers in your awareness. If your awareness is free of hidden wounds, false beliefs, and fixed attitudes, the way to fulfillment of desire is clear. Once it is born, a new desire has no difficulty reaching the result you want, because you have achieved the result first in consciousness. By the same token, if there are obstacles along the way, your desire will meet those obstacles in manifest form. So if you want to fulfill desires smoothly and with the least effort, clear the way as much as possible in your own awareness. Every bit of negativity that you release will make outward life that much closer to the spiritual ideal of complete abundance.

I will honor every part of myself in its proper place.

This affirmation is about balance. People are surprised to encounter a great deal of chaos when they go inside. Not only is the mind restless and wayward, the ego offers its own agenda. Having touched on the ego's needs to assert its demands, one shouldn't have the impression that it is an enemy. The ego has its proper place. The same holds true for the mind with its confusing stream of jumbled ideas, beliefs, desires, fantasies, and emotions. Its chaos poses problems when you try to see your soul clearly, yet the mind has an enormous capacity to perceive reality in new ways. In their proper place, mind and ego are to be cherished as allies. Remind yourself of this in the long campaign to bring balance back to your inner world. Ego and mind will seem to fight against you, but in truth they harbor their own spiritual goals, not to rule over the soul but to be absorbed in its domain of light. One of the best ways to allow your ego to be absorbed in spirit is to witness it silently. You do this by just observing your own reaction to situations, circumstances, people, and events. In the mere witnessing of these, you will begin to see a transformation, and a balancing of body, mind, and spirit.

DAY 64

I will learn the difference between ego and spirit.

This affirmation is about the need to discriminate true from false. Your ego wants to gain from the soul—too eagerly, in fact. Once you turn its attention toward spirit, your ego mistakes it for another race to win, another goal to accomplish, another result to achieve. In other words, it translates everything spiritual into terms it can understand. On a mass scale we witness this tendency when people hate and go to war in the name of God. They co-opt spirit to justify their selfish agendas. There is no escaping this tendency, because until it reaches the end of life's journey and gets absorbed into the soul, your ego will never stop assuming that the path is for the glory of itself. "I am enlightened" is just as selfish a statement as "I know how to win." Your soul is the one thing ego will never win for you, thus it is essential to learn to distinguish the ego's values from the values of the true self.

I ask for detachment.
I will not confuse it with indifference.

This affirmation is about how to end attachment. The ego, having learned that the soul is detached, has a hard time ending its habit of clinging to external things. If you keep firm in your resolve not to be selfish and acquisitive, the ego resorts to a second, subtler line of defense. It turns indifferent. In place of wanting money, status, and possessions, it says that nothing matters. This is a disguised form of clinging, however, because indifference is a mask. It manifests as withdrawal, but it is actually a call for attention. It later evolves into self-denial in which the "I" is attached to holiness, righteousness, and austerity. This way to God remains self-centered even though material wealth has been renounced. The soul's version of detachment doesn't mean that material comforts may not be part of your life. It simply means that you do not cling to them with anxiety. Detachment comes when there is such fullness of spirit inside that you don't feel any need to acquire.

I ask for inner peace.
I will not mistake it for withdrawal.

This affirmation is about avoiding spiritual depression. One looks around and notices many spiritually sincere people who don't look happy. In some cases their depression is self-inflicted; they feel that God condemns desire, therefore they punish themselves for having needs, wants, wishes, and dreams. They try to achieve an emotional flatness that barely participates in the world. Other forms of spiritual depression exist because the person believes that God wants us to withdraw from life and all its disturbances. You can find a kind of peace by withdrawing, but it is the ego's peace, born of a decision to avoid all conflict, to renounce anger as bad and unworthy of a spiritual person, to escape all taint of negativity as it exists "out there." You must learn to avoid these tactics of the ego by seeing that inner peace also extends outward. It comes from embracing creation as divine in every aspect. When you are not afraid of anything, you can unite with it. In union you attain a peace that nothing "out there" can shake.

I ask for wisdom.

I will not confuse it with information.

This affirmation is about certainty. Because the mind is constantly seeking answers, each of us wants to know with certainty about God, the soul, death, and the afterlife. With enough data, the mind assumes it will finally know the answer to cosmic questions. But data is external; facts can only deliver information. There is nothing alive in either, and the soul is life itself. It nourishes a kind of knowledge that constantly renews itself and shapes its understanding to the eternal present. We call this wisdom. People who believe they are wise because they have lived a long time and have accumulated much experience have confused wisdom with acquisition. You can't acquire wisdom as a possession; you can only expand until the wide embrace of your mind includes enough spirit that it has changed you inside. As the Vedas say, "This is the kind of knowledge you turn into."

I ask to surrender.

I will not confuse it with giving up.

This affirmation is about loss. When you surrender, you give up something that once you had a personal stake in. Because there is a loss, the ego sees this as giving up. From the perspective of "I, me, mine," loss is unacceptable. Having set down its strategy for living, the ego remains committed to it. Surrender involves giving up such cherished beliefs as "I must be right," "I must be in control," "I must be strong," along with many other aspects of the ego's strategy. The aim of the ego is personal survival and the triumph of your self as an isolated, strong, independent person. These aims are not the opposite of spirit's aims, yet they are too limited. When you surrender, you are giving up a small world to gain a much greater one. As is said in the Indian tradition, you are giving up a hut to live in a palace.

I ask for strength.
I will not confuse it with control.

This affirmation is about power from within. Spirit brings power. That is a paradox, because the spirit's path to power involves surrender, humility, forgiveness, and acceptance—not exactly qualities we associate with powerful people. In the ego's world, power means having the ability to control circumstances to your benefit, to manipulate or dominate people in order to get your own way. If what you want is the greatest good for everyone, ego has little to say. The kind of strength that is giving, selfless, devout, trusting, and patient is decidedly feminine. It belongs to saints and mothers. By affirming this kind of strength, you are demonstrating faith that there can be power without aggression, domination, and control. Is there real power in the feminine aspect? Certainly there is, and even though the ego has exercised control for a long time, spiritual power has always been in charge. Spiritual power pervades every aspect of life as the intelligence that nurtures and organizes all forms, atom to cosmos. This power is yours to tap into. It comes from inside, and nothing can stop it once you have found its source in the true self.

I ask for acceptance.

I will not confuse it with resignation.

This affirmation is about allowing. Tolerance faces resistance from critics who believe that if you allow too much freedom, human nature will become wild, lawless, and destructive. What would have happened, they charge, if the great monsters of evil in history had been allowed to have their way? Here one needs to see the difference between passivity and acceptance. Someone who accepts you doesn't simply let you do whatever you want. Spirit doesn't ask anyone to resign themselves to evil and wrongdoing. When evil actions or attitudes arise, we have a duty to assert our sense of justice. Yet even as we hate the sin, we do not hate the sinner. In that distinction the meaning of acceptance can be grasped. Acceptance means you see the equality of souls. You allow for the truth that spirit abides in everyone. Hard as it may be for moralists to believe, a sinner may act out of suffering rather than evil. His wrongs may be a call for love and understanding. All people deserve those things. Even if their actions lead to punishment, that doesn't invalidate their higher status as children of God.

I will seek to undo my sins without attacking myself as a sinner.

This affirmation is about redemption. Many people who have a strong moral sense find it hard to correct the sin and not the sinner. The voice raised against a wrong somehow keeps going and wants the person to be redeemed as well. At bottom this aim is not just pointless but impossible. Actions are redeemed by exchanging bad for good. You undo the wrong and pay your debt. If you try to save your soul in the process, you miss the truth that it is the soul that is out to save you, not the other way around. Because guilt drives us to correct our sins (defined in a nonreligious sense as consciously wrong actions) it is often held as a positive emotion. Taken too far guilt is extremely destructive, however. Like many other energies, such as fear and anger, guilt will not willingly go away once it is let out of the box. It prefers to deliver its guilty verdict over and over, long past the time when any useful purpose had been served. The most moral people tend to suffer over trivial sins, or over no sin at all. Therefore repudiate any impulse to attack yourself. This habit of self-torture will never lead you to your soul but only keep you in deeper isolation.

I ask for fulfillment.
I will not confuse it with pleasure.

This affirmation is about what it means to be happy. It is natural for the ego to seek pleasure, thinking that once it is found, happiness is the result. Pleasure is not an antidote for pain, however. If you are suffering, no amount of pleasurable experience from the outside will relieve your anguish. This disproves the ego's assumptions, but still there is no need to renounce pleasure. Instead we have to acknowledge that happiness comes from another source. What is that source? It is the unchanging essence that lies within.

As the ancient sages declared, we all know what it's like to wake up from a dream. Spirit is known just as easily. After you experience a moment of waking up to it, the dream of pleasure becomes unreal. This waking up needs to occur over and over. You need to notice those instances of alert, joyful, alive, free, unbounded being. They come and go, but not like the things that change all around us. Essence comes and goes like the sun, which once free of clouds, can be seen to shine constantly.

DAY 73

I will heal separation by seeing through its illusions.

This affirmation is about going beyond the perception of separation and seeing the reality of unity consciousness. Even though it may seem that you are separate from your source or from God, you are not. The perceived separation is the cause of all suffering. This illusion isn't real, but it is convincing. Beneath the pain that we all experience is a level of being which is independent of both pleasure and pain. This is the level that is referred to as the peace that passes all understanding. When you get in touch with this level of your existence your suffering will begin to ease.

DAY 74

I will break through the illusion of helplessness.

This affirmation is about the healing intention. When you intend to accomplish something, you set things in motion within yourself. An intention to walk, for example, activates the motor centers of the brain along with balance, heart rate, blood pressure—in fact, the whole mind-body system goes into walking mode. Healing works exactly the same way. Unlike walking, however, the intention to heal requires a transformation that can only be brought about by spirit, for spirit controls all energies, including those in your body. When you intend to heal, you break down the illusion of helplessness. To do so, clearly visualize your intended outcome. This could be increased physical and mental capacity, energy, vitality, enthusiasm for life, and a sense of connection with the creative power of the universe, joy, and love. Nurture this intended outcome in your heart. Let it incubate through meditation, and soon you will be inspired to make choices that will allow you to step out of helplessness and into a state of inner strength and power.

I will break through the illusion of denial.

This affirmation is about confronting reality. As long as you look the other way, illusion persists, so you must pay attention. Do this by sitting quietly and with firm but gentle resolve ask for your true feelings to come forward. Be with any source of pain in your body. Feel it directly, no matter where it is. Now ask the pain of every kind to gather in your heart. As it gathers, ask each aspect of suffering to name itself. Be as specific as possible.

Having defined specifically the exact emotion you are experiencing, whether it is fear, anger, guilt, or depression, express the origins of this feeling to yourself through writing or journaling. Be careful not to use the language of victimization. Once you have completed this task, share these feelings with someone you can trust. Next you may release them through a ritual of your own devising—such as dancing, or burning the papers on which you have written down your experiences. Finally, celebrate the release of this blocked energy. Instead of denying your suffering, which only prolongs it, now you have defined, expressed, shared, released, and celebrated it—and moved on.

DAY 76

I will break through the illusion of dependency.

This affirmation is about receiving help. When you are weak-ened by pain and suffering, the fear of becoming dependent on others grows. This is a natural fear. It's important to pre-serve a sense of personal dignity, yet finding and receiving help is absolutely necessary. In every crisis, suffering can be alleviated at the energy level. But you don't have to assume the whole burden yourself. To access deeper, more stubborn energy, ask for guidance. For some people, the presence of spiritual guides such as angels, masters, saints, deities, *boddhisatvas*, and deceased loved ones brings reassurance and help. Intend that helpers come to you in any form and at any time. Then remain alert and follow the hints that spirit gives you. You are being heard. Your soul is able to guide you to any help that you need. Ultimately, no matter who responds to you, it is your own true self responding.

I will break through the illusion of numbness.

This affirmation is about giving yourself permission to grieve. Grief is a wrenching emotion and therefore one of the most threatening. Those we love have been taken inside us and made a part of who we are. When they die or are threatened by crisis, we feel that our own being has been attacked. To the unconscious mind, there is a real threat that we are going to die with them. By going numb instead of grieving, your ego pretends that the loss isn't agonizing, that the threat is not so grave as it actually is.

Grief falls into the rare category of being a necessary suffering. You have to go through it before you can release it back to the light. Have patience with your grief. In this period of necessary suffering comes a great sense of purification. The sting of death is no longer quite as anguishing. The possibility of letting in the light once again becomes real.

Day 78

I will break through the illusion of emptiness.

This affirmation is about the holes that suffering creates. The ache of loss is difficult to bear, and often the worst part is the fear that nothing exists behind the ache except a void. Know that emptiness is an illusion. No matter how much you have suffered, your soul sees you as whole. Affirm today that you share this vision and have the intention to allow the light of spirit to come in and fill any voids it may find. To aid in this repair, close your eyes and see white light surrounding you like a bubble or cocoon. Visualize the light filling the entire space within you, seeking out rifts, tears, holes, and gaps. Ask for these to be completely filled with light.

I will break through the illusion of being abandoned.

This affirmation is about loneliness. One of the worst parts of suffering a great loss is the feeling of utter isolation. The problem of loneliness, which exists for countless people, requires deeper healing than simply seeking out company. Loneliness can happen in a crowd and may feel most intense when you find yourself alone on a packed city street. As a child it was easier to cure loneliness, because the presence of a parent was enough to offer reassurance. As an adult, loneliness becomes more existential—it feels as if you have been abandoned, yet you cannot say by whom. If you suffer from loneliness, have the intention to befriend yourself; ask for spirit to comfort you with its presence, inviting it in with the meditation on the heart *(Day 54).* End it by sitting quietly and asking to be allowed into the refuge of your heart. Feel your heart as a soft, warm enclosure; settle there with your attention, and rest as long as you wish. If you repeat this technique enough times, you will find that the presence of spirit is very real and accessible.

I will break through the illusion of despair.

This affirmation is about receiving love. There is a kind of suffering that remains mute and unspoken. It grows from the belief that you are unloved. Children need constant reassurance that they are loved because their sense of self is undeveloped and therefore fragile. By hearing "I love you," they gain a core of self-worth. As long as this core is strong, a person can withstand the loss of love, even though it may bring intense pain. When the core of self-love has become too weak, despair is the result. In some people it was never strong enough to begin with; in others the intensity of grief has proved too much. Ask spirit to come in and repair your innate sense of being loved. In one of the most famous Upanishads there is a line, "It is not for the sake of the beloved that you feel love, but for the sake of the self." Giving and receiving are two halves of one circle. Grief breaks this circle apart. Affirm today that you can feel loved within yourself, even after a great loss.

I will renew myself by having no expectations.

This affirmation is about accepting the unknown. Today you
are stepping into the unknown by letting go of expectations.
When you hold on to an expectation and it fails to come true,
unhappiness is the automatic result. At a subtler level, the fact
that you put your faith in expectation blocks the arrival of new
energies. This is true whether you expect a positive outcome
or a negative one. "It will all work out somehow" feeds off
expectation as much as "Nothing good will ever come of this."
Affirm that you do not need expectation. See it as a form of
control rooted in fear. If you expect nothing, you can put your
faith in the now, the only place that is endlessly renewed.

I will renew myself by releasing the ghosts of the past.

This affirmation is about memory. Suffering is a tangle of the past, present, and future. You have no need of either the past or the future when you step fully into the present. Memory loses its power to harm, not by forgetting old wounds but by living so fully in the now that such wounds become irrelevant. By affirming that you will release all ghosts from the past, you vanquish a host of ills. Recall an earlier point: remembering pain and holding on to it is anger. That is only the beginning. Remembering pleasure and holding on to it is addiction. Anticipation of pain or pleasure in the future is anxiety. The redirection of past pain at oneself is guilt.

Although it may seem that you are feeling distress in the present, if you dive deep into the now you will be so absorbed that pain cannot intrude. The present is the home of your being—past and future are only the dreams of what you were or what you might become. So affirm today that you will release the past and its burden of wounded dreams.

I will renew myself by letting go of self-importance.

This affirmation is about not being offended. When someone says or does something that offends you, the hurt isn't being felt by you but by your self-importance. Self-importance comes about because we all carry a self-image inside ourselves. We spend huge amounts of time and energy defending this phantom. If your image depicts you as a person of refinement and education, you will be offended by coarseness. If your image is that of someone in control, an authority, you will be offended when someone with less status acts like your equal. If you want renewal, self-image must be released. Bring yourself into the present without any image. Let your responses to events flow with the same ease and freedom as life itself. Realize that as long as you are attached to self-importance you will always feel offended. Affirm to yourself that relinquishing self-importance is your ticket to freedom.

DAY 84

I will renew myself by letting go of resentment.

This affirmation is about realizing there is no such thing as a missed opportunity. "I should have done that" and "If only I had said that" bring to mind all our failures, big and small. Resentment wastes energy, yet it lingers seductively because it always comes with a ready-made target. The alternative is to look inward, mourn what might have been, take responsibility, and move on. Your soul sees no missed opportunities. In reality every road you traveled offered up an experience as a gift, and as the complex fabric of life wove itself, each experience added to your growth. In the deepest sense your life has been a string of opportunities that you met successfully. So affirm today that there is nothing and no one to resent. For every small desire that didn't come true, your soul has widened the way for fulfilling your highest aspirations.

DAY 85

I will express my faith through prayer.

This affirmation is about trusting in your vision. Right now you are only aware of spirit in glimpses. You sense your soul for a while, and then it vanishes again. Through faith you hold on to the ultimate vision. Prayer links who you are now with who you will be.

> *God and Spirit, I pray to keep my vision ever before me.*
> *I ask you to bless my journey.*
> *I ask your divine helpers to protect me along the way.*
> *I ask my inner guides to lead me forward.*
> *I pray to the soul that is within, without, and everywhere*
>   *that I may know myself as holy, and as whole.*
>   *Amen.*

Say this prayer at the start of your day. Sit or kneel with eyes closed and go inward to feel the words coming from your heart. This prayer will be heard at the source, which is the union of yourself and God.

DAY 86

will pray to be new again.

This prayer is about releasing confusion. Every day we must find some way to ask spirit for clarity. Tailor the prayer below to your own needs by specifically naming what you are confused about. Is it who to trust? Is it how to be understood and heard by others? Is it the inability to make a choice when more than one direction attracts you—or do there seem to be no choices at all?

Asking for clarity opens the way for everything spirit wants to bring you. Without clarity, you wouldn't be able to notice or receive its messages.

God and Spirit, I'm in a fog today.
Give me clarity in mind and heart.
Release me from my confusion, which is born of the past.
Let me see everything as if for the first time.
Shower unknown blessings upon me,
Surprise me with joy,
And let me be renewed in your ways.
        Amen.

DAY 87

I will pray to remember who I am.

This prayer is about knowing yourself as spirit. We all wear many guises and have many selves. Our ultimate self—spirit, soul, essence—plays the most mysterious role. It speaks with a silent voice. It brings messages that seem new and strange compared to our old patterns of thinking. It asks for restraint when the ego is ready to leap into action. Yet this mysterious presence is truly who we are. Today's prayer asks for a reminder when you are tempted to forget the reality of the true self.

God and Spirit, I forget who I am today.
Remind me.
Let me hear the voice of silence.
Let me see what cannot be seen.
Let me feel your faintest touch.
I know that you are as close as my breath.
So breathe in me today.
     Amen.

/ will pray to forgive.

This prayer is about asking to feel more than you feel. Forgiveness belongs to the heart. You can understand its value, you can believe that it is moral, good, upright, and righteous to forgive—but if you don't feel it, forgiveness is forced. Spirit sees everything from a place of total balance. Countless times you have needed forgiveness; countless times you have offered it to someone else. The mantle of who is right and who is wronged gets passed around in a circle. When you cannot find in yourself the purity of forgiveness, ask to feel more than you feel. Spirit won't give you new and better reasons to forgive someone. It will show you another way.

God and Spirit, I am hard of heart today.
There is someone I cannot forgive.
My own hurt blocks the way.
I feel the sting of being wronged.
Take this stiffness from my heart,
Let me feel the joy of tenderness.
Restore peace and lift the energy of grievance.
Let me truly forgive as I would be forgiven.
     Amen.

I will pray to show my love.

This prayer is about letting others see you as you truly are. At many points on the spiritual path you will feel exalted and holy. You will know without a doubt that spirit is in you. But showing this to others is difficult. Should you behave like a saint? Should you wait until your family notices that a holy person is sitting at the dinner table? Goodness is shown through good works, but spirit is transmitted through love. Without expecting anything from anyone, find a way to express the exaltation that you feel inside.

> *God and Spirit, show your love through me.*
> *This is all I want or have ever wanted.*
> *Make a secret pact with me.*
> *Let someone in my life feel your touch*
> *As I feel it myself:*
> *Intimate, tender, joyful, and healing.*
> *When this happens, don't let them see me,*
> *But only you.*
> *No one needs to know that I am in you and you in me.*
> *We'll keep our secret until eternity.*
>> *Amen.*

I pray to live beyond "I" and "Thou."

This prayer is about being in the world but not of it. Beyond the duality of the material world, all divisions end. The only relationship worth having is with God, because when you relate to other people, you see God in them. This state of grace is what today's prayer asks for. Use it when the world is too much with you, when you feel that God or spirit or your soul stand too far apart. Let the sweetest and most intimate relationship, which is between "I" and "Thou," melt into the same river of wholeness.

God and Spirit, I ask to take your hand in mine.
I have seen this world through your eyes.
I have loved others as you would love them.
I have entered creation and played to my heart's content.
But for all that, I miss you.
Be mine without end.
Accept me like a drop melting back into the ocean.
I've known everything but eternity.
As I give myself to you,
Give that to me.
    Amen.

I will find my refuge in spirit.
The only safe place is eternity.

This affirmation is about being. The river of life flows between the banks of pleasure and pain. If you feel stuck on the bank, rejoin the flow and it will carry you beyond. Practice acceptance in place of force, letting life bring things to you and take them away again. Keep your eye on being, which is reality. Whatever comes before you, observe it for what it is. Remember, you are not what happens, no matter how intense it may be. You are the one it is happening to. When "I" is safe in its own being, the world loses all fear.

We are endlessly renewed in each other,

therefore no one ever dies.

This affirmation is about communion. When the spiritual path winds through time and space, you walk it as a single body, a single personality, and a single ego. These are garments you put on when you began your journey, only to take them off again now at its end. If this is so, then who is making the journey? No one and everyone. Although we exchange identities at the moment of death, shedding one "I" to put on another, at the source there is only being, unmoving, eternal, ever the same, giving life to each fragment of itself yet never gaining or losing. In the cycle of endless renewal, your speck of eternity is inviolate. As we live in our being, none of us ever dies.

To be healed is to be holy. To be holy is to be whole. To be whole is to know that all selves are the same "I."

This affirmation is about the end of yearning. In India it has been taught for centuries that the soul has two faces. One face is turned toward God and knows itself as being made of the same holy essence. The other face is turned toward creation, and although it knows itself as divine, it can experience birth and death. The eternal face is Atman; the face that accepts birth is Jiva. Although they are both aspects of your soul, without Jiva you would never have left God and eternity to enter your body. Without Atman you would never know that something sacred lies behind the mask of the material world. I often marvel at the ingenuity of grace, which contains infinity in the finite, bliss inside pain, clarity despite the fog, love despite conflict. This is God's magic act, to make us so that we will be both born and undying. Today you are affirming that you have seen through the illusion. The magic has entertained you enormously, but now you've seen how the trick works. In the end, once Jiva has gained every drop of spirit that the world has to offer, the division is no more. Jiva merges into Atman. The soul has only one face, again and forever.

Evil is the absence of being.

This affirmation is about the darkness and the light. Just as the soul has two faces, so does Nature as a whole. We are in the habit of calling these two faces good and evil, life and death, the darkness and the light. But as convincing as that picture is, duality exists only to keep Maya, or illusion, going. The instant anything was born it had to die. These two events became the material symbol for light and darkness. The illusion breaks down when you realize that just as God has only one essence, reality has only one face, which is being.

At the deepest level being fills everything. But if you know that, then the drama of life and death wouldn't be convincing. Evil derives from the illusion that the divine has gone away. In itself evil has no positive claim to existence. The illusion ends when your soul reveals that being is everywhere, and you are that being. Realizing this, no one can adopt evil ever again. It becomes an old role that means nothing when the drama has worn itself out.

I will express my being as joyful play.

This affirmation is about the true purpose of life. As long as the drama of good versus evil, pleasure versus pain, keeps its appeal, the purpose of life is struggle. Duality, being born of separation, exists as a stage set. Since the drama is so full of richness, what do we do when it ends? Is all purpose lost when there's nothing more to win or lose? Many people are horrified at the prospect of giving up duality. As someone once candidly told me, "Go back into the light? It sounds an awful lot like death to me!"

The purpose of life after you escape duality is joyful play. This has always been the purpose. Your senses cannot tell that pain is just another form of bliss—they think it is the opposite of pleasure. But once you know yourself as spirit, play becomes divine. The light knows that there is nothing but itself. So why should any aspect of itself be less than joyful? Unlike pleasure, bliss is an eternal feeling, born of the sheer enjoyment of creation with itself.

When all is me and mine, there is only love.

This affirmation is about redeeming the ego. Ego, too, gets redeemed. Only then do you realize what an amazing trick God has pulled, to make the villain of the piece its final hero. When you see that you are pure being, separation ends. The gap between you and your soul is closed and—presto!—everything in creation belongs to you. In one stroke you fulfill the ego's reason to exist, not by defeating it but by giving it what it wants. Individual ego rises to the status of cosmic ego. Looking in all directions, you see only being, which is yourself. The experience shatters the ego's fear and loneliness. Ego may be the last to see that all it wanted was God's love, yet in the end it does. In the healing of separation, love becomes real, never to be taken away. Just as the ego shared your purpose when life was a struggle, it can now share your new purpose, which is joyful play. The drama of light and dark, it turns out, was a romantic comedy all along.

The world is my body.

The mountains are my bones; the forests are

my skin; the rivers are my blood; the air is

my breath; the sun is my sight.

In my love for the earth, I balance all life.

This affirmation is about the unseen role of being. In its detachment the soul performs no actions. Yet it has entered everything. The physical matter of the cosmos has been expressing spirit at every instant since the Big Bang. Behind the random motion of swirling superheated gases, a hidden purpose was playing itself out. Being was upholding life. In the swirling gases was enclosed the creation of DNA, of all plants and animals, of the entire complex design we call evolution. As the choreographer, being didn't step onstage. It guided the dance from without. Once you see yourself as this same being, you have the joy of guiding the dance from within. In the expansion of your own awareness, you radiate the same life-enhancing influence as spirit itself.

I am all bodies, all thoughts, all emotions, all breathing, all situations, all circumstances, all events, and all relationships. I embrace all.

This affirmation is about uniting two realities. There is a path to God that relies solely on the mind. It is the coldest, rockiest road, offering nothing of comfort to the heart, yet the path of the mind is also the simplest. It sets out to answer one question: Who am I? The instant you ask the question, only two answers emerge, diverging like two roads in the woods.

The first answer: "I am this mind and body, born in the physical world and destined to die."

The second answer: "I am being itself, which gives rise to the cycle of birth and dying but lives eternally beyond them."

No one ever takes the second road, nor I believe are we meant to. If you could satisfy yourself mentally that you are the eternal "I," what would be the use of experience? This world was made to be the most enticing, seductive, beautiful, intoxicating, erotic, and sensual part of creation. It begs to be experienced, and therefore we all took the first road. We put on individuality and subjected ourselves to birth and death. The drama has been magnificent. Pleasure and pain have overwhelmed us. Yet if birth and dying were the ultimate reality, the road would lead to hell, so by the grace of being, the first road simply dissolves. The second road remains eternal. The being that is unborn and never dies, appears. You know the truth of who you are, which is All. Birth and dying go on. But you can step outside the drama whenever you wish. You can reclaim yourself beyond pleasure and pain. With undying gratitude you look back over your shoulder and realize that for you suffering has come to an end.

DAY 99

I affirm my life as life itself.
I affirm my love as love itself.

This affirmation is about enlightenment. At the end of the journey lies a state of absolutes. Freedom isn't being free from this or that—it is absolute freedom. Joy isn't joy in this or that—it is absolute joy. So it is with power, intelligence, creativity, and existence. When we experience these things in duality, we are gaining only a faint flavor of them. From the perspective of the relative world, the absolute is unimaginable. The ancient sages could only define it by negation: unborn, undying, unmoving, impenetrable, and invulnerable, without any quality and yet having every quality.

At the outset I said that suffering is the pain that threatens to take away meaning. So in my own personal vision of the end of the spiritual path, I don't see an end at all. Meaning continues to expand eternally, and it does this through those two divine forces we call life and love. The end of suffering comes at that precise instant when you can say, "I am life, and I am love." Your awareness merges into creation as the observed, the observer, and the act of observation. Others have imagined God as an eye overlooking Creation, including every atom in its gaze. This may be so, but for me this gaze will not be divine unless it looks with love. Love ignites the spark of life and gives it a worth that is infinite.

The only reality is love.

This affirmation crystallizes all those that have come before. Read the following lines, allowing them to lead you into a state of meditative peace. Let the words enter your heart and soothe it with reassurance.

In my garden the rose opened, but I was in too much of a hurry and passed it by. Love remembered me and said, "I will make a rose bloom in your heart. Your body is the garden of the soul."

Having read these words, consider the priorities in your life. Love is the only reality. When this truth takes root in your heart, you will not be tempted to waste so much time on trivialities. Stake your life on what is timeless, and you will be redeemed.

I couldn't sleep for the ache in my heart.

I was anxious and had thoughts of dying.

Then I saw a figure made of light standing

by my bed. He said, "Only one thing could

make you suffer this much." He bent to kiss

me, and I knew that my lover was the soul.

Deepak Chopra and The Chopra Center for Well Being at La Costa Resort and Spa, Carlsbad, California, offer a wide range of seminars, products and educational programmes, worldwide. The Chopra Center offers revitalizing mind/body programmes, as well as day spa services. Guests can come to rejuvenate, expand knowledge or obtain a medical consultation.

For information on meditation classes, health and well-being courses, instructor certification programmes, or local classes in your area, contact The Chopra Center for Well Being at La Costa Resort and Spa, 2013 Costa Del Mar Road, Carlsbad, CA 92009, USA. By telephone: 001-888-424-6772, or 001-760-931-7566. For a virtual tour of the Center, visit the Internet website at www.chopra.com.

If you live in Europe and would like more information on workshops, lectures or other programmes about Dr. Deepak Chopra or to order any of his books, tapes or products, please contact: Contours, 44 Fordbridge Road, Ashford, Middlesex, TW15 2SJ (tel: +44 (0) 208 564 7033; fax: +44 (0) 208 897 3807; email: sales@infinite-contours.co.uk; website: www.infinite-contours.co.uk).

If you live in Australia and would like more information on work-shops, lectures, or programmes presented by Dr. Deepak Chopra, please contact What's On The Planet Pty Ltd, PO Box 161, Brighton Le Sands, NSW 2216, Australia, or email deepak@theplanet.com.au.

If you have enjoyed this book and would like the opportunity to explore higher realms of consciousness, you may do so interactively at Deepak Chopra's new website, www.mypotential.com.

Rider books are available from all good bookshops or by ordering direct on 01624 677 237. Or visit our website at www.randomhouse.co.uk.